I0028201

COOPERATIVE BUSINESS LAW

A Practical Guide to the Special Laws Governing Cooperatives

3rd Edition 2020

Michael W. Droke

*with contributing authors from
Dorsey & Whitney LLP*

Copyright © 2020 by Dorsey & Whitney LLP

All rights reserved. This book or any portion thereof may not be reproduced or used in any manner whatsoever without the express written permission of the publisher except for the use of brief quotations in a book review.

Printed in the United States of America

First Printing, 2014

Second Edition Printing, 2014

Third Edition Printing, 2020

ISBN-13: 978-0-9914055-4-1

DORSEY™
always ahead

Table of Contents

Introduction

The field of cooperative business law has expanded as the use of this unique corporate structure extends into new business areas. Farmers, grocers, retailers, workers, and others seek the benefits of the cooperative culture while maintaining operational flexibility and risk management. This practical guide helps board members and executives understand the many and varied legal issues that can arise when serving a cooperative and its members.

Cooperatives often act, and are treated from a legal perspective, like all other types of corporate business entities. Rather than providing a comprehensive summary of general business law principles, this manual contains topics that are suitably covered in condensed format. It focuses primarily on legal treatment unique to the cooperative structure and areas where general principles operate differently because of the cooperative structure. The chosen format is designed principally to heighten awareness and facilitate discussion of these and other subjects.

Michael W. Droke, Partner
DORSEY & WHITNEY LLP

This guide is published for general information purposes only. This guide does not provide legal opinions or advice, and should not be relied up on as such. No attempt has been made to address all of the legal issues involved in cooperative business management, or to treat any one issue comprehensively. While cases and statutes have been updated as of the date of publication, the law in this area changes; therefore, one should always consult an attorney with regard to the legal implications of any particular situation.

CHAPTER I
WHAT IS A COOPERATIVE?

Section 1.1   Statutory Definition

What is a cooperative, and how is it different from other corporate forms? Most corporate entities are owned by either private individuals or shareholders, whose primary interest is to obtain a profit from the corporation's activities. A cooperative has a different ownership structure, with legal and practical ramifications. At its most basic, a cooperative is a business structure in which the owners (often called "members" or "patrons")[1] are limited to those who also use the cooperative's services, market products through the cooperative's sales efforts, or buy the cooperative's goods.[2] The members have a financial interest in the co-op[3]; but they also have a strong interest in the co-op's continued service, sales or purchasing success.

A cooperative, sometimes called a "cooperative association," is a type of corporation organized under state statutes and which satisfies certain organizational and operational requirements to be treated as a cooperative for

---

[1] Some statutes define who is or can be a "patron." *See* CAL. CORP. CODE § 12243(a). California law also defines "patronage" in the same section.

[2] This book also discusses an emerging form called Limited Cooperative Associations ("LCAs"). LCAs allow minority interest by financial stakeholders. *See*, Section 1.8.

[3] For example, California law requires proportional and equitable sharing of earnings based on "patronage." CAL. CORP. CODE § 12201. The concept of patronage is discussed throughout this book, particularly in Chapter CHAPTER II.

federal income tax purposes. Like for-profit corporations and limited liability corporations ("LLCs"), cooperatives are distinct legal entities from their owners. In other words, the "corporate shield" applies. The key distinguishing feature is that cooperatives are owned and controlled by the people or entities that use the cooperative's services. They finance and operate the business or service of the cooperative for the mutual benefit of members, reaching objectives that would be unobtainable acting alone.

The definition of a cooperative is generally very broad. It can include any cooperative association, society, company or exchange.[4] The law does not require capital stock (shares) or any specific name. However, some states only allow business entities organized as a cooperative to use the word "cooperative" as part of their name.[5]

Section 1.2   Cooperative Principles

The concept of a cooperative form of business began in the 1840s with the establishment of the Rochdale Society of Equitable Pioneers.[6] That society began with a set of principles that have been developed over time. Many organizations (both cooperatives and those who serve them) have identified specific attributes of a cooperative.

---

[4]   *See, e.g.*, WASH. REV. CODE § 23.86.010. For additional states' definitions of "cooperative," *see* CAL. CORP. CODE § 12232; MINN. STAT. ANN. § 308A.005 subdiv. 5; OR. REV. STAT. § 62.015(4); WIS. STAT. § 185.01(1).

[5]   *See, e.g.*, CAL. CORP. CODE § 12311(b); MINN. STAT. ANN. § 308A.011; OR. REV. STAT. § 62.850; WASH. REV. CODE § 23.86.030(2); WIS. STAT. § 185.94.

[6]   *See* "Cooperative." *Encyclopedia Britannica Online.* Encyclopedia Britannica Inc., last updated 6-11-2014, *available at*: http://www.britannica.com/EBchecked/topic/136330/cooperative; *see also* David Thompson, *Co-op Principles Then and Now (Part 2)*, Cooperative Grocer Network (Jan. 9, 2004), http://www.cooperativegrocer.coop/articles/2004-01-09/co-op-principles-then-and-now-part-2.

Key concepts include:

- Open and non-discriminatory membership opportunity.

- Democratic membership control over the cooperative. This often is expressed by the "one member, one vote" philosophy for centralized (individual member) cooperatives, and democratic control for cooperatives with other entities as members. Democratic control is both the strength of the cooperative form, and the element that most complicates its day-to-day operation.

- Equitable and democratic sharing of gains, so that most of the investment capital is common property of the cooperative, and most net-revenue or profit is distributed pro rata to members based on their use of the cooperative, subject to operating reserves.

- In fact, many marketing cooperatives exist not to make a "profit," but rather to increase member revenues through joint selling programs. Purchasing cooperatives may exist to decrease member costs through increased bargaining power rather than make a "profit" to distribute. As a result, the incentive, organizational and operating structure of the cooperative can be very different from typical profit-based corporations. As described throughout, cooperatives must still make sufficient margin in order to have the cashflow to operate. However, the leftover margin is redistributed back to the members through patronage.[7]

• Education and training for members and staff, as well as the general public on the basis and benefits of the cooperative form.

• Autonomy and independence, focusing on the ability to develop the cooperative solely for the continued independence of the cooperative and democratic control of its members.

Section 1.3   Why Not Other Corporate Types?

Groups wanting to establish a cooperative should carefully consider the alternative corporate structures before establishing the entity. As noted above, many cooperatives do not exist to create a "profit" in the classic sense.[8] Member and staff motivations can be very different than those in for-profit corporations. That being said, unless an organization is organized under a cooperative statute many states will not allow the use of the term in the organization's name – even if organized in another state.[9]

For-profit corporations are typically formed to capitalize on an idea or service to generate profit for the company's owners. Cooperatives are formed for different reasons.

Marketing cooperatives are often formed to combine volumes to increase sales leverage or maximize the ability to develop a brand from commodity products. Purchasing cooperatives are formed to decrease costs

---

[7]   *See* CAL. CORP. CODE § 12244.

[8]   *See*, Rapp & Ely, *How to Start a Cooperative*, USDA Cooperative Info. Report No. 7, www.rurdev.usda.gov/rbs/pub/cir7/cir7.pdf.

[9]   In California, the cooperative may use the word in its name, while an entity organized under a different code section cannot use the word "cooperative" in its name. CAL. CORP. CODE § 12311. For other state examples, see Appendix E.

through increased buying power. They can also secure more predictable supply or obtain access to supply or markets that are too expensive for individual members.

As discussed in other chapters, many of the benefits of the cooperative structure are available to properly-organized corporations. For example, the tax benefits available to cooperatives may be open to other forms if done correctly. [10] Cooperative founders should consider whether the member-incentive focus of a cooperative is better than the profit-incentive focus of other corporate forms.

> ### PRACTICAL TIP
>
> *Consider the reasons the form is attractive to your organization and whether other corporate forms are superior before starting the cooperative. Will democratic control by users be a benefit, or will it make decision making more difficult? Will absence of profit at the cooperative level help the members, or be a disincentive to management? Are there other corporate entities such as limited liability corporations that have similar tax benefits, but without some of the limitations imposed by cooperatives (Chapter II)? Are the financing limitations imposed on cooperatives too onerous (Chapter V)?*

Section 1.4   Types of Cooperatives

While the broad statutory language of many state cooperatives statutes permits many types of cooperatives, most fit into a few distinct categories.

---

[10]   *See* Chapter II.

(a)   Purchasing

Joint purchasing can give cooperative members a consistent supply of goods, with greater purchasing power, cost management, and inventory control. In some cases, purchasing cooperatives enable members to buy products or services unobtainable on a smaller scale, and reduce costs when profits are redistributed to members. Purchasing cooperatives must carefully monitor their (and their members') actions to comply with antitrust regulations.

(b)   Marketing

Combining volume produced by cooperative members can give greater sales leverage and create recognizable brands that would be unattainable by members acting alone. Marketing cooperatives can improve bargaining power, reduce costs (through purchasing agreements and discounts), obtain or broaden market access, and improve distribution and service.

(c)   Federated

Cooperatives can have members that are other cooperatives as well. A "federated cooperative" is a separate legal cooperative whose membership is comprised entirely of other cooperative organizations.

(d)   Hybrid

In addition to federated cooperatives, some are organized with a membership base that includes both subsidiary cooperatives and other types of members as well. For example, Land o'Lakes is a hybrid cooperative with a membership base of ranchers and subsidiary cooperatives. Like a corporation whose stock is owned by companies and individuals, a hybrid cooperative can be a flexible vehicle to enable entry into multiple markets. However, both federated and hybrid cooperatives must carefully monitor their status as antitrust-exempt organizations.[11]

(e)   Agricultural

Many agricultural producers band together to help organize smaller farms into cooperative associations that can more easily and efficiently perform overhead functions that would be too expensive to do individually.[12] For example, ranchers often band together to purchase, warehouse and locally ship feed products. Wheat farmers band together to aggregate and sell their wheat. Farmers also set up purchasing cooperatives to obtain fuel, other agronomy, or supplies.

(f)   Consumer Cooperatives

Many consumer businesses are organized as cooperatives, including natural foods cooperatives and other retail cooperatives.[13] Consumer cooperatives can be as small as a local coffee shop, or as large as Recreational Equipment, Inc. (REI).

(g)   Electric/Power Distribution

Rural and metropolitan groups have organized to form electric and power distribution cooperatives across the

---

[11] *See* Chapter VII for discussion and analyses of the Capper-Volstead Act of 1922.

[12] Many state cooperative statutes expressly authorize agricultural cooperatives. *See* MINN. STAT. ANN. § 308A.101 subdiv. 1; WASH. REV. CODE § 23.86. Other state statutes permit cooperatives to be organized "for any lawful purpose" except banking and insurance. *See, e.g.,* CAL. CORP. CODE § 12201; OR. REV. STAT. § 62.115; WIS. STAT. § 185.03.

[13] *See* WASH. REV. CODE § 24.06.005, *et seq.;* CAL. CORP. CODE § 12201, *et seq.*

United States.[14] There are over 900 such cooperatives in operation.

(h)   Fisheries

Fisheries and fish processors have organized both marketing and purchasing cooperatives in order to expand their branding and production capacity.[15]

(i)   Housing

Housing cooperatives have sprung up to help smaller groups organize to purchase larger housing projects.

(j)   Insurance

Captive insurance companies may be eligible to be organized as a cooperative.[16]

(k)   Worker Cooperatives

Cooperatives operating in many business sectors are organized with the employees as patrons, contributing labor and management services.[17]

---

[14] Many state cooperative statutes expressly authorize electric cooperatives. *See* MINN. STAT. ANN. § 308A.101 subdiv. 2; WASH. REV. CODE § 23.86.400(b). Other state statutes permit cooperatives to be organized "for any lawful purpose" except banking and insurance. *See, e.g.*, CAL. CORP. CODE § 12201; OR. REV. STAT. § 62.115; WIS. STAT. § 185.03.

[15] U.S. Dep't of Agriculture, Agricultural Cooperative Service, Research Report No. 44, Fishery Cooperatives, *available at*: www.rurdev.usda.gov/rbs/pub/rr44.pdf(1985).

[16] *See, e.g.*, WASH. REV. CODE § 23.86.022. Some state cooperative statutes, however, do not permit insurance cooperatives. *See, e.g.*, OR. REV. STAT. § 62.115; WIS. STAT. § 185.02.

[17] *See* CAL. CORP. CODE §§ 12201.5, *et seq.*; 12253.5.

(l)   Credit Unions

Credit unions, while exempt from tax under Section 501(c)(14) of the internal revenue code (if state chartered) or under federal law (if federal chartered), operate on a cooperative basis for the mutual benefit of their member depositors and borrowers.

(m)   Other

A cooperative can be created by any group of individuals or businesses wishing to collaborate. Farmers markets, artists, and others have created cooperative business associations owned by the members they serve.

Section 1.5   Powers

Cooperatives resemble most other businesses. They can own property, hire employees, enter into contracts, and engage in most other business transactions as an entity separate from their members.[18] State cooperatives statutes generally give cooperatives broad powers to engage in business activities. For example, in Washington State, cooperatives' powers include the following:[19]

- To have perpetual succession by its corporate name unless a limited period of duration is stated in the articles of incorporation.

- To sue and be sued, complain, and defend in its corporate name.

- To have and use a corporate seal.

- To purchase, take, receive, lease, or otherwise acquire, own, hold, improve, use, and deal in and

---

[18] *See generally* CAL. CORP. CODE § 12320; MINN. STAT. ANN. § 308A.201 subdiv. 1; OR. REV. STAT. § 62.125; WASH. REV. CODE § 23.86.035; WIS. STAT. § 185.03.

[19] WASH. REV. CODE § 23.86.035.

with real or personal property or any interest therein, wherever situated.

- To sell, convey, mortgage, pledge, lease, exchange, transfer, or otherwise dispose of all or any part of its property and assets.

- To purchase, take, receive, subscribe for, or otherwise acquire, own, hold, vote, use, employ, sell, mortgage, lend, pledge, or otherwise dispose of, use, and deal in and with shares or other interest in, or obligations of, other domestic or foreign corporations, associations, partnerships or individuals, or direct or indirect obligations of the United States or any other government, state, territory, governmental district or municipality, or any instrumentality thereof.

- To make contracts and incur liabilities, borrow money at rates of interest the association may determine, issue notes, bonds, certificates of indebtedness, and other obligations, receive funds from members and pay interest thereon, issue capital stock and certificates representing equity interests in assets, allocate earnings and losses at the times and in the manner the articles of incorporation or bylaws or other contract specify, create book credits, capital funds, and reserves, and secure obligations by mortgage or pledge of any of its property, franchises, and income.

- To lend money for corporate purposes, invest and reinvest funds, and take and hold real and personal property as security for the payment of funds loaned or invested.

- To conduct business, carry on operations, have offices, and exercise the powers granted by the

Cooperative Business statute, within or without Washington state.

- To elect or appoint officers and agents of the corporation, define their duties, and fix their compensation.

- To make and alter bylaws, not inconsistent with its articles of incorporation or with the laws of this state, for the administration and regulation of the affairs of the association.

- To make donations for the public welfare or for charitable, scientific, or educational purposes, and in time of war to make donations in aid of war activities.

- To pay pensions and establish pension plans, pension trusts, profit-sharing plans, stock bonus plans, stock option plans, and other incentive plans for any or all of its directors, officers, and employees.

- To be a partner, member, associate, or manager of any partnership, joint venture, trust, or other enterprise.

- To cease corporate activities and surrender its corporate franchise.

- And, as a catch-all, to have and exercise all powers necessary or convenient to effect its purposes.

PRACTICAL TIP

Cooperative bylaws are often very simple as compared to other corporate forms. They are often designed as a membership communication tool. Some cooperative bylaws are two pages or less. Unlike articles of incorporation, bylaws can be modified by a majority vote of the board of directors. Therefore, they sometimes contain broad discretionary powers granted to the board. See discussion below.

Section 1.6   Articles of Incorporation

All cooperatives must adopt written articles of incorporation[20] and should adopt bylaws outlining the rights and responsibilities of the organization.[21] Articles of incorporation may be changed only by vote of the members as a whole, while bylaws can be changed by a majority of the board of directors. As a result, articles of incorporation tend to create broad rights and responsibilities that are unlikely to be modified, while bylaws are often more detailed.

For example, in California and Washington, the articles must contain the following elements:[22]

- The name of the association.

- The purpose for which it was formed, which may include the transaction of any lawful business for

---

[20]   *See, e.g.,* CAL. CORP. CODE § 12310; MINN. STAT. ANN. § 308A.131; OR. REV. STAT. § 62.513; WASH. REV. CODE § 23.86.050; WIS. STAT. § 185.05.

[21]   *See, e.g.,* CAL. CORP. CODE § 12330-12331; MINN. STAT. ANN. § 308A.165; OR. REV. STAT. § 62.135; WASH. REV. CODE § 23.86.100; WIS. STAT. § 185.07.

[22]   *See* WASH. REV. CODE § 23.86.050. For examples of required elements in the articles of incorporation under other state statutes, *see* MINN. STAT. ANN. § 308A.131; CAL. CORP. CODE § 12310.

which associations may be incorporated under this chapter. It shall not be necessary to set forth in the articles of incorporation any of the corporate powers enumerated in this chapter. California law requires the following statement: "This corporation is a cooperative corporation organized under the Cooperative Corporation Law. The purpose of this corporation is to engage in any lawful act or activity for which a corporation may be organized under the law."[23]

- Its principal place of business.

- The term for which it is to exist, which may be perpetual or for a stated number of years.

- If organized without capital stock, whether the property rights and interest of each member shall be equal or unequal; if unequal, the articles shall set forth the general rules by which the property rights and interests of all members shall be determined and fixed. The association may admit new members who shall be entitled to share in the property of the association with old members in accordance with the general rules.

- If the association is to have capital stock, the articles should state:

  o The aggregate number of shares which the association shall have authority to issue; if shares are to consist of one class only, the par value of each share, or a statement that all shares are without par value; or, if shares are to be divided into classes, the number of

---

[23] CAL. CORP. CODE § 12310 contains the required elements for cooperative Articles of Incorporation. CAL. CORP. CODE § 12313 contains permissive elements.

shares of each class, and a statement of the par value of the shares of each class or that shares are to be without par value.

o If the shares are to be divided into classes, the designation of each class and a statement of the preferences,[24] limitations, and relative rights in respect to the shares of each class.

o If the association is to issue the shares of any preferred or special class in series, the designation of each series and a statement of the variations in the relative rights and preferences between series fixed in the articles of incorporation, and a statement of any authority vested in the board of directors to establish series and fix and determine the variations in the relative rights and preferences between series.

o Any provision limiting or denying to members the pre-emptive right to acquire additional shares of the association.

• Provisions for distribution of assets on dissolution or final liquidation.

• Whether a dissenting member shall be limited to a return of less than the fair value of the member's equity interest in the association. A dissenting member may not be limited to a return of less than the consideration paid to or retained by the association for the equity interest unless the fair value is less than the consideration paid to or retained by the association.

---

[24] CAL. CORP. CODE § 12245.2; *see also* CAL. CORP. CODE § 12246.2. Classes of members may have different voting rights. CAL. CORP. CODE § 12253(b).

- The address of its initial registered office, including street and number, and the name of its initial registered agent at the address.

- The number of directors constituting the initial board of directors and the names and addresses of the persons who are to serve as the initial directors.

- The name and address of each incorporator.

- Any provision, not inconsistent with law, which the incorporators elect to set forth in the articles of incorporation for the regulation of the internal affairs of the association.

- Any provision eliminating or limiting the personal liability of a director to the association or its members for monetary damages for conduct as a director to the extent permitted by state law.

- Any provision which under the Cooperative Business Act is required or permitted to be set forth in the bylaws.

Copies of the articles of incorporation must be filed with the Secretary of State.[25] State statutes generally permit amendment of the articles by a majority vote of the members voting on the amendment at any regular meeting or at any special meeting called to vote on the amendment.[26] However, state statutes may require that the total vote on the proposed amendment exceed a certain percentage of

---

[25]   *See* CAL. CORP. CODE § 12300; MINN. STAT. ANN. § 308A.131 subdiv. 2; OR. REV. STAT. § 62.511; WASH. REV. CODE § 23.86.055; WIS. STAT. § 185.043.

[26]   *See, e.g.,* CAL. CORP. CODE § 12502; MINN. STAT. ANN. § 308A.135; OR. REV. STAT. § 62.560; WASH. REV. CODE § 23.86.090. The Wisconsin cooperatives statute, however, requires the approval of two-thirds of the members to amend the articles of incorporation. WIS. STAT. § 185.52.

the cooperative's total membership or impose other requirements for voting on amendments. Approved amendments to articles of incorporation are then recorded with the Secretary of State.

> ### PRACTICAL TIP
> *Articles of Incorporation are like the cooperative's constitution. They are typically short, technical, and establish broad rights of members. They can contain protections against hostile takeover. They can limit meeting rights. Cooperatives should periodically (but no less than every 5 years) review their articles of incorporation to determine if they should be updated or amended.*

Section 1.7   Bylaws

As noted above, the cooperative's bylaws are based upon the articles of incorporation, but because they are easier to modify often contain much greater detail establishing the corporate structure. Various state statutes either permit or regulate what can be contained in a cooperative's bylaws. For example, a cooperative, through its bylaws, can specify which qualifications a director must possess, or require directors to be residents of a particular state, shareholders of the cooperative, or both. Absent such a directive, a director need not be a state resident or a shareholder of the corporation under state law.[27]

Often, the bylaws significantly define member rights and responsibilities. Bylaws can include requirements for membership[28]; duties of membership; rights of classes of stock; timing, location and number of annual meetings;

---

[27] WASH. REV. CODE § 23B.08.020.
[28] CAL. CORP. CODE §§ 12238, 12331.

procedures for special meetings; and procedures to elect members of the board of directors. Bylaws also outline the voting rights of types and sizes of members. For example, members can be divided into groups, classes, regions, districts, or other classifications for governance purposes.[29]

Bylaws document the essential relationship between the cooperative and its members. Because the members are also the customers of the cooperative, the bylaws should be created with customer relationships in mind. A cooperative's strength comes from the close relationship of the members to each other, and to the cooperative. They should be carefully drafted to ensure fair treatment among members and between the members and the board. They should also be drafted in a format and style that is easy for the members to understand.

Some jurisdictions allow bylaws to be adopted or amended by the board, without action by the members. Some states impose limitations on the right of the board to amend bylaws without membership approval.[30] Urgent business pressures sometimes require amendment before the timeline of membership meetings and approvals can be met. Therefore, many cooperatives permit bylaw amendments by board action without member approval, subject to limitations set by statute or the Articles of Incorporation or the bylaws themselves.[31]

---

[29] CAL. CORP. CODE §§ 12223, 12230, 12331.

[30] CAL. CORP. CODE § 12330. This statute allows bylaw amendments by the board unless certain conditions apply. For example, a board could not amend the bylaws in a way that materially and adversely affects member voting rights on specific major decisions. Likewise, members are allowed to amend the bylaws, but with restrictions if the amendment materially alters rights of a particular class.

[31] See CAL. CORP. CODE § 12330(c, d).

Bylaws are a main governing document. They can be short or long, detailed or plain English. Most states allow significant flexibility on what the bylaws can contain. For example, California's Cooperative Associations Act includes references to bylaws regarding:

- Membership admission requirements. .[32]

- Rights to assess dues, assessments, or fees on members.[33]

- Rights to require members to pay a capital contribution.[34]

- Membership voting power rules, if permitted by the articles of incorporation.[35]

- Membership interest transfers and rights, including escheatment (transfer to state) and hypothecation (mortgage).[36]

- Membership rights to indivisible reserves accounts for non-patronage income.[37]

- Rules required to be included in the bylaws by the articles of incorporation.[38]

- Any provisions authorizing the board to issue restrictions or limitation on rights or privileges of

---

[32] CAL. CORP. CODE §§ 12403, 12404 (membership transfer limitations), 12420 (different types or classes of membership), 12421 (equality of membership rights), 12422 (redemption rights), 12423 (resignation of membership).

[33] CAL. CORP. CODE § 12441.

[34] CAL. CORP. CODE §§ 12442, 12454 (restrictions on purchase or redemption of shares).

[35] CAL. CORP. CODE § 12301; *see also* CAL. CORP. CODE § 12246.2. Classes of members may have different voting rights. CAL. CORP. CODE § 12253(b).

[36] CAL. CORP. CODE §§ 12446, 12520.

[37] CAL. CORP. CODE § 12454.5.

[38] CAL. CORP. CODE § 12313.

unissued shares,[39] and to issue shares without payment (called "consideration").[40]

- Any limitations on the board to act on behalf of the cooperative.[41]

- Rights to amend the bylaws by the board or membership, or limitations on right to amend without membership approval (in some cases requiring super-majority vote to amend).[42]

- Statements setting the number of board members, methods to approve selection, expansion, removal, vacancy, and replacement of board positions. Examples include voting for board members by proportional voting, by class, or the like.[43]

- Limitations on indemnification of board members.[44]

- Rights of members to delegate authority.[45]

- Bylaw inspection rights and duties, and rights to other information.[46]

- Board meeting procedures.[47] While the bylaws can be flexible in some ways, certain limitations apply. For example, special meetings "shall" (mandatory, not permissive) be called upon 4

---

[39] CAL. CORP. CODE §§ 12313(6) and (7).

[40] CAL. CORP. CODE § 12400.

[41] CAL. CORP. CODE §§ 12320, 12350, 12375 (loans to board members).

[42] CAL. CORP. CODE § 12330.

[43] CAL. CORP. CODE §§ 12331, 12333, 12360 (term), 12361 (vacancy due to, for example, missed meetings), 13262 (filling of vacancies, resignations).

[44] CAL. CORP. CODE § 12377.

[45] CAL. CORP. CODE § 12332.

[46] CAL. CORP. CODE §§ 12340, 12591 (information rights and annual reports), 12952 (disclosure of indemnification agreements to members and directors).

[47] CAL. CORP. CODE § 12351.

days mailed or 48 hours' in person notice. "The articles or bylaws may not dispense with notice of a special meeting."[48]

- Committee establishment, appointment, duties, and limitations.[49]

- Officer positions, duties, qualifications, and termination provisions.[50]

- Membership certificates requirements.[51]

- Membership meetings, including allowing meeting notice by electronic or other means.[52] This section also addresses special meeting requirements, and meetings called by the membership rather than the board.

- Quorum requirements.[53]

- Bylaw provisions in a merger or acquisition.[54]

- Distributions and liquidation of assets.[55]

The comprehensive list of possible topics permitted under California law is comparable to the flexibility embedded in most other state statutory schemes. Many of these provisions are *permissive*, not mandatory. In other words, the cooperative's bylaws does not need to have each of these elements. Most rights can be modified in the bylaws, but there are some important exceptions (for example, setting minimum notice requirements for special

---

[48] CAL. CORP. CODE § 12351(a)(2).
[49] CAL. CORP. CODE § 12352.
[50] CAL. CORP. CODE § 12353.
[51] CAL. CORP. CODE § 12401.
[52] CAL. CORP. CODE §§ 12460, 12463 (actions by written ballot in lieu of meeting), 12481 (setting record date for membership meeting rights), 12482 (joint memberships and voting rights of joint members).
[53] CAL. CORP. CODE § 12462.
[54] CAL. CORP. CODE § 12531.
[55] CAL. CORP. CODE §§ 12657, 12658 (winding up).

meetings). While some cooperatives might want to copy bylaws from others in their industry, one size does not fit all cooperatives. Competent legal and tax counsel should be consulted when adopting or modifying the bylaws, and for periodic review.

> **PRACTICAL TIP**
>
> *Cooperative bylaws are the essential governance document. They should be clearly written with the interests of the members in mind.*
>
> *If permitted by statute, bylaws should also be subject to amendment by the board without membership approval. This allows for flexibility and responsiveness when needed due to urgent business pressures.*
>
> *Bylaws should be given to each board member annually. They should also be reviewed annually by management, the board, and legal/tax counsel to determine if amendments are appropriate.*

Section 1.8   Limited Cooperative Associations and Other Options

In the past two decades, a new type of cooperative business entity that allows for non-patron investor-members has emerged in several states. Limited Cooperative Associations ("LCAs"), as they are called, are substantially similar to other types of cooperatives in most respects.[56] Most of the LCAs are patterned after the Uniform Limited Cooperative Associations Act ("ULCAA").[57]

---

[56] Exhibit B is a compilation of the states which permit Limited Cooperative Associations.

[57] LIMITED COOPERATIVE ASSOCIATION ACT (Unif. Law Comm'n 2007), https://www.uniformlaws.org/committees/community-home?Community Key=22f0235d-9d23-4fe0-ba9e-10f02ae0bfd0

LCAs subscribe and adhere to the core cooperative attributes developed since the establishment of the Rochdale Society of Equitable Pioneers (the "Rochdale Principles"). They are member owned, democratically governed, and are intended to grow and operate sustainably for the benefit of their members.

LCAs have the flexible governance structures of modern limited liability corporations ("LLCs"). For example, in 2019 Washington state enacted a LCA that sets forth default rules, but allows the LCA to establish its own set of "organic rules" of governance.[58] Additionally, they are required to operate on a cooperative basis and may use the word "cooperative" in their name.[59]

Unlike traditional cooperatives, a member of an LCA need not be a patron, but instead can be an investor who does not patronage the co-op. By allowing non-patron investors to become members, LCAs have more capacity to generate financing than the traditional cooperative. LCAs can entice investors with voting rights. The maximum voting power of investor-members varies by state, and is often capped at a minority of the governing body. Investor-members receive revenue allocations proportionate to the ratio of their investments to those of other investors.

To ensure that the balance of power in the LCA does not shift in favor of investor-members, the patron-

---

[58] WASH. REV. CODE § 23.100.0109. This section lists the items that may be varied either by the Articles of Incorporation, or Bylaws. It also requires the "organic rules" to address member contributions. WASH. REV. CODE § 23.100.0109(4).

[59] See, e.g., WASH. REV. CODE § 23.100.0113. In California, the cooperative must use the word in its name, while an entity organized under a different code section cannot use the word "cooperative" in its name. CAL. CORP. CODE § 12311.

members are given certain protections. Those protections can include: capping the percentage of profits allocated to investor-members, mandating that patron-members control the majority of the vote, and requiring a majority of patron-member votes to approve any action.[60]

> ### *PRACTICAL TIP*
>
> *LCAs are similar to, but different from, other types of cooperatives. While flexible in structure, they do not have the taxation, antitrust and other protections needed. Patron-members might object that the LCA is not a "true co-op," even if it is operating on a cooperative basis.*

---

[60] *See also*, Section 2.4 and Section 7.3.

CHAPTER II
UNIQUE TAX RULES FOR
COOPERATIVES

Christopher R. Duggan

Section 2.1   Introduction

The most important requirements imposed on cooperatives are those contained in the federal income tax laws.
These laws define the conditions for qualification as a
cooperative for federal tax purposes and the procedures
under which cooperatives can deduct patronage distributions from their income. Because few cooperatives could
survive as cooperatives if their earnings were taxed twice
(once at the cooperative level, and again at the patron
level), cooperatives must carefully comply with the federal tax requirements to qualify for single tax treatment.

The primary source of federal tax rules governing cooperatives is Subchapter T of the Internal Revenue Code of
1986, as amended (the "Code"). Subchapter T comprises
just eight sections of the Code, Sections 1381 to 1388,
and defines various types of patronage distributions and
the tax treatment of such distributions. Though Subchapter T was enacted only in 1962, it codified cooperative requirements developed since the 1920s from rulings
of the Internal Revenue Service (the "IRS") and the

courts. Other federal income tax requirements for cooperatives are found in the Treasury Regulations, federal
court decisions, and IRS documents like Revenue Rulings, Revenue Procedures and private letter rulings.
These non-statutory tax authorities need to be inter-
preted with some care because the IRS has abandoned
many requirements that it formerly applied to cooperatives.[61]

Before discussing the specific federal tax rules governing
cooperatives, it is useful to understand the theory underlying these rules. This theory arose in the 1920s and
1930s, well before the enactment of Subchapter T, and
was formulated in IRS rulings addressing the definition
of "income" for purposes of the federal corporate income tax.[62] Then, as now, cooperatives were required by
their governing documents to calculate their income each
year from patronage business and to distribute this income to patrons based on the amount of business each
patron conducted with the cooperative. The IRS rulings
viewed mandatory cooperative patronage distributions
of this sort as "corrective and deferred price adjustment[s]" to the prices at which the cooperative did business with its members.[63] Because a cooperative was legally bound to return these price adjustments or "re-
funds" to patrons, these amounts were never owned by,

---

[61]   Among others, these rules have recently been abandoned by the IRS: (1) the rule
that capital gains constitute *per se* non-patronage-sourced income, (2) the rule that
cooperatives cannot pay ordinary dividends exclusively from non-patronage income (the so-called "dividend allocation rule"), (3) the rule that a cooperative cannot carry forward or backward a net operating loss, (4) the rule that a cooperative
must do more than 50% of its business with members, and (5) the rule that non-
exempt cooperatives are "membership organizations" subject to the restrictions
of I.R.C. § 277.

[62]   *See* the discussion in Christopher R. Duggan, "Chief Counsel Advice 201228035:
A Critique," *The Cooperative Accountant* (Fall 2013) 62-71.

[63]   Rev. Rul. 61-47, 1961-1 C.B. 193; Rev. Rul. 54-10, § 3.04, 1954-1 C.B. 24.

and could not be taxed to, the cooperative.[64] In technical terms, the IRS treated cooperative patronage distributions as an "exclusion" rather than a deduction from cooperative income.[65] Though Subchapter T describes patronage distributions as "deductions" in its provisions, it incorporates all the requirements of prior law which cooperatives needed to meet in order to exclude patronage dividends from their income.[66]

> ### PRACTICAL TIP
>
> *Cooperative taxes are complicated and different from other corporate forms. Unlike most other corporations, income from member activity is not taxed to the cooperative. This results in significant tax savings, since income is only taxed once, rather than twice (to the cooperative, then the member). Of course, the IRS places strict limitations on which entities can get this preference. Many of the tax requirements ensure that the cooperative is indeed acting in accordance with cooperative principles, such as limited profit and democratic control. The significant savings requires cooperatives to carefully comply with tax rules. Cooperatives must find good tax and legal counsel who understand both how cooperatives work, and how income is taxed.*

---

[64] *E.g., Harbor Plywood Corp. v. Commissioner*, 14 T.C. 158, 161 (1950) ("the patronage dividends are at all times the property of the member stockholders and nonmembers"); I.T. 3208, 1938-2 C.B. 137 (the amount of patronage dividends "was not includible in gross income of the corporation").

[65] Rev. Rul. 61-47, 1961-1 C.B. 193; *Pomeroy Cooperative Grain Corp. v. Commissioner*, 31 T.C. 674, 686 (1958), *overruled by* 288 F.2d 326 (1961).

[66] *See* Duggan, "Chief Counsel Advice 201228035."

Section 2.2   Qualification as a Cooperative Under Subchapter T

Subchapter T applies to (1) tax-exempt farmers' cooperatives qualifying under Code Section 521, and, with certain specified exemptions,[67] (2) "any corporation operating on a cooperative basis."[68] Section 521 farmers' cooperatives are subject to strict limitations with respect to membership and the conduct of their business, and they enjoy few benefits beyond that of non-exempt cooperatives. Because few cooperatives now attempt to qualify under Section 521, and many existing Section 521 cooperatives have given up their tax-exempt status, the discussion below focuses exclusively on non-exempt cooperatives.

A prospective cooperative must first qualify as a corporation for federal tax purposes in order to avail itself of treatment under Subchapter T. For purposes of Subchapter T, all corporations formed under state corporation acts meet this requirement – there is no need for the corporation to be formed under a state cooperative statute. In fact, many non-exempt cooperatives have been formed or reincorporated under a state general business corporation statute in order to avoid the often burdensome requirements of state cooperative acts.[69] Subchapter T does not apply to partnerships; nor does it apply to most limited liability companies. Prospective cooperatives should be aware that entities created under

---

[67] The exceptions include tax-exempt organizations and cooperative organizations covered by other Code provisions, such as mutual savings banks, mutual insurance companies, and rural electric and telephone cooperatives.

[68] I.R.C. § 1381(a).

[69] Cooperatives formed under state general business corporation acts must ensure that their articles and bylaws include an obligation to pay patronage dividends, limitations on dividends and liquidation proceeds paid on capital stock, and a requirement that unallocated equity be distributed based upon historical patronage.

certain state cooperative statutes (called Limited Cooperative Acts or "LCAs") constitute partnerships by default for federal income tax purposes.[70] An entity formed under such a statute will not qualify for Subchapter T unless it makes a timely and valid election to be treated as a corporation under the federal check-the-box rules.

The second requirement for treatment under Subchapter T is that the corporation must be "operating on a cooperative basis."[71] This phrase is not defined in the Code or the Treasury Regulations, and its meaning turns on case law and IRS rulings. The most important definition of operating on a cooperative basis is found in *Puget Sound Plywood, Inc. v. Commissioner*, wherein the Tax Court established three requirements: subordination of capital, democratic control and operation at cost.[72]

(a)   Subordination of Capital

The "subordination of capital" requirement requires that state law or the organizational documents of the cooperative place strict limits on the financial return on the stock of the cooperative in order that "ownership of the pecuniary benefits" arising from the cooperative's operation belong to the patrons.[73] This requirement prevents

---

[70] Examples of state cooperative statutes that create a partnership entity for federal income tax purposes include, but are by no means limited to, the following acts: (1) The Iowa Cooperative Associations Act, Iowa Code § 501A, (2) The Minnesota Cooperative Associations Act, Minn. Stat. ch. 308B, and (3) Wyoming Processing Cooperative Law, WYO. STAT. § 17-10-201 *et seq.* A list of such statutes is included as Appendix E.

[71] I.R.C. § 1381(a)(2).

[72] *Puget Sound Plywood, Inc. v. Commissioner*, 44 T.C. 305, 308, 322 (1965).

[73] *Puget Sound*, 44 T.C. at 308. As formulated by the *Puget Sound* court, the subordination of capital principle also requires members to have "control over the management and direction of the cooperative" such that members "have the right and power to elect the trustees and the officers of the cooperative." 44 T.C. at 308. Because this requirement is analytically part of the democratic control requirement, it is addressed below in the discussion of that requirement.

a cooperative from paying more than a fixed dividend on its stock, generally no more than 8%.[74] The subordination of capital requirement also requires that, upon liquidation or redemption, an equity holder in the cooperative can receive no more than the stated dollar amount of his equity.[75] Accordingly, a corporation operating on a cooperative basis cannot issue common stock; all equity in the cooperative must be strictly limited in its claims to cooperative income and assets.

(b)   Democratic Control

The "democratic control" principle requires a cooperative to maintain a policy of one-member, one-vote or a patronage-weighted voting policy. The *Puget Sound* court indicated that democratic control is generally satisfied by having the members "periodically assemble in democratically conducted meetings at which each member has one vote and one vote only, and at which no proxy voting is permitted."[76] The IRS subsequently relaxed this requirement by authorizing proxy voting and mail-in ballots.[77] In addition, both the IRS and the Tax Court have held that voting in accordance with patronage satisfies the democratic control requirement, unless such policy results in

---

[74] I.R.S. Priv. Ltr. Rul. 2011-41-007 (Oct. 14, 2011) (8% dividend is consistent with the subordination of capital requirement); *United Cooperatives, Inc. v. Commissioner*, 4 T.C. 93,106 (1944) (8% dividend is consistent with cooperative operation).

[75] *See, e.g.*, I.R.S. Priv. Ltr. Rul. 2012-08-008 (Feb. 24, 2012) (subordination of capital requirement met where the liquidation proceeds would be distributed only up to the par value of preferred stock); I.R.S. Priv. Ltr. Rul. 2011-41-007 (Oct. 14, 2011) (subordination of capital requirement met where only class of stock is "limited upon dissolution").

[76] *Puget Sound*, 44 T.C. at 308.

[77] *See* Rev. Rul. 75-97, 1975-1 C.B. 167 (permitting proxy voting); I.R.S. Priv. Ltr. Rul. 2002-10-033 (Mar. 8, 2002) (permitting voting by mail-in written ballots).

de facto control of the cooperative by af small group of patrons/investors.[78]

The democratic control requirement does not require a cooperative to give any voting or governance rights to non-members, including non-members treated as patrons.[79] This is because the purpose of the democratic control requirement is to prevent mere stockholders or investors from exercising control over the cooperative, not to ensure patron democracy.[80] Because of this purpose, the IRS has not ordinarily (if ever) challenged the cooperative status of an association on democratic control grounds unless such association was controlled by investors.[81]

The IRS has treated voting rights under the democratic control requirement as the right to elect members of the board of directors.[82] Cooperatives should consult with an

---

78 *See Thwaites Terrace House Owners Corp. v. Commissioner*, 72 T.C.M. (CCH) 578 (1996) (permitting voting rights in a housing cooperative that varied in accordance with the size of the member's housing); I.R.S. Tech. Adv. Mem. 7408193090D (Aug. 19, 1974) (patronage-based voting is acceptable within limits); I.R.S. Gen. Couns. Mem. 38,061 (Aug. 22, 1979) (permissible to use "limited patronage voting (*e.g.*, a maximum of 5 percent of the total vote allowed to any one member)," but "unlimited patronage voting can lead to abusive situations"). Despite this authority, the IRS will not issue a private letter ruling that a corporation is operating on a cooperative basis unless the corporation has a one member, one vote policy.

79 *See, e.g.*, Rev. Rul. 72-602, 1972-2 C.B. 510 ("There is no requirement that in order for an organization to obtain the benefits of a nonexempt cooperative under Subchapter T that both members and nonmembers be treated equally."); I.R.S. Priv. Ltr. Rul. 2011-41-007 (Oct. 14, 2011) (cooperative satisfied democratic control requirement even though "participating patrons" had no right to vote).

80 *See, e.g.*, *Keystone Automobile Club Casualty Co. v. Commissioner*, 122 F.2d 886 (3d Cir. 1941) (involving a cooperative that was a mutual insurance company).

81 *See, e.g.*, *Etter Grain Co., Inc. v. United States*, 462 F.2d 259 (5th Cir. 1972) (questioning the status of an association as a cooperative where five owners of preferred stock held voting control); I.R.S. Tech. Adv. Mem. 7408193090D (Aug. 19, 1974) (cooperative failed democratic control requirement because voting structure gave investors excessive control); A.O.D. 1990-07 (Feb. 20, 1990) (disagreeing with court decision on grounds that cooperative violated democratic control requirement by granting voice in management only to shareholders).

82 *See, e.g.*, I.R.S. Priv. Ltr. Rul. 89-37-019 (June 19, 1989).

experienced cooperative attorney if they wish to appoint or limit voting for certain director positions, or if they wish to restrict the nomination of directors.

(c)   Operation at Cost

The "operation at cost" principle requires that a cooperative distribute its patronage income to patrons on a patronage basis. The *Puget Sound* decision describes this basis as "the *proportionate* vesting in and allocation among the members of all *fruits* and *increases* arising from their cooperative endeavor." [83] With respect to annual income ("fruits"), this requirement is satisfied if the cooperative distributes income from business with patrons in accordance with the patronage dividend requirements in Subchapter T (discussed below).[84] With respect to appreciation in value ("increases"), this requirement is satisfied if the cooperative's organizational documents require that the cooperative, upon liquidation, must distribute liquidation proceeds in excess of the stated dollar amounts of equities in accordance with historical patronage.[85] Except in certain circumstances, it is permissible for a cooperative's liquidation clause to limit liquidating distributions to members and to calculate distributions based upon patronage over the previous 10 years.[86]

---

[83] *Puget Sound*, 44 T.C. at 308 (emphasis added).
[84] *See* I.R.C. § 1388(a) (definition of patronage dividend); I.R.S. Priv. Ltr. Rul. 2012-08-008 (Feb. 24, 2012); I.R.S. Priv. Ltr. Rul. 2011-41-007 (Oct. 14, 2011).
[85] *See, e.g.*, Rev. Rul. 70-481, 1970-2 C.B. 170 (liquidation proceeds must be distributed to pay the par or stated value of stock and patrons' equities and then "to the members on the basis of their past patronage")
[86] Rev. Rul. 72-36, 1972-1 C.B. 151 (liquidation proceeds must be distributed on the basis of historical patronage "insofar as is practicable").

Section 2.3 Cooperative Operations Under Subchapter T

Subchapter T provides the rules that permit a cooperative to avoid entity-level federal income tax. The primary method for cooperatives to avoid such tax is the distribution of "patronage dividends" in the manner prescribed by Subchapter T. Other less common means under Subchapter T for cooperatives to avoid federal income tax, such as the use of "per-unit retain allocations" and the redemption of "nonqualified written notices of allocation," are briefly addressed later in this chapter.

It should be noted that the Subchapter T rules apply to "patrons," which is a broader category than "members." A "patron" is "any person with or for whom the cooperative association does business on a cooperative basis, whether a member or a non-member of the cooperative."[87] For this purpose, a cooperative is deemed to do business with a person "on a cooperative basis" if it does such business under an obligation to pay patronage dividends to the person based on that person's business with the cooperative. This terminology recognizes that many cooperatives are authorized by their organizational documents to pay patronage dividends to non-members if the non-member enters into a patronage agreement with the cooperative.

(a) Definition of Patronage Dividend

Under Subchapter T, a "patronage dividend" is an amount paid by a cooperative to a patron that: (1) is based on the quantity or value of the business done with or for the patron, (2) is paid pursuant to an obligation by the cooperative to pay such amount, which obligation

---

[87] Treas. Reg. § 1.1388-1(e).

existed before the cooperative received the amount, and (3) is based on the net earnings of the cooperative from business done with or for patrons.[88] Each of these characteristics deserves some explanation.

PRACTICAL TIP

Cooperative members know and love their patronage dividends! However, not all income to the cooperative is a "patronage," so some profit may be subject to double taxation. Each time a cooperative enters a new line of business, management should review whether it can be organized to generate patronage-based net income for tax purposes.

(i)   Pre-Existing Obligation

A patronage dividend must be paid by the cooperative pursuant to a pre-existing obligation. This obligation distinguishes a patronage dividend, which substantively is a rebate, from an ordinary dividend. All cooperative bylaws must include language that requires the cooperative to pay patronage dividends, and cooperatives should be careful that amendments to its bylaws do not inadvertently weaken or eliminate this language. It is well-established, however, that a cooperative's organizational documents can authorize the board of directors to divert a small portion of its patronage-sourced income (10-15%) to pay stock dividends or to create a reserve fund without eliminating the pre-existing obligation with respect to the percentage of income that *could* have been diverted.[89] Any amount actually diverted pursuant to such provision, of

---

[88] I.R.C. § 1388(a).
[89] *See. e.g.,* Rev. Rul. 69-621, 1969-2 C.B. 167.

course, could not be used to pay a patronage dividend and would be subject to tax at the cooperative level.

(ii)   Patronage-Sourced Income

A patronage dividend also must be paid from income from "business done with or for patrons," *i.e.* "patronage-sourced income." Patronage-sourced income clearly includes income from business done directly *with* patrons, *i.e.* sales to patrons and purchases from patrons. Patronage-sourced income also clearly *excludes* income from transactions with non-patrons if the transactions are "substantially identical" to transactions done with patrons.[90] In short, if a cooperative engages in substantially identical business transactions with both patrons and non-patrons, it cannot use income generated by its business with the non-patrons to pay patronage dividends to the patrons.

In addition to income from cooperative business done *with* patrons, however, patronage-sourced income also potentially includes business done *for* patrons, (provided the income does not come from substantially identical transactions). The test applied by the IRS and the courts is that the income must come from activities that are "directly related to" or that "actually facilitate" the marketing, purchasing or services activities of the cooperative.[91] Under the directly related/actually facilitates test, "[t]ransactions with third parties that are reasonably related to the business which a cooperative conducts

---

[90] *See* I.R.C. § 1388(a), which provides that patronage dividends do not include amounts paid by a cooperative from income "from business done with or for other patrons to whom no amounts are paid, or to whom smaller amounts are paid, with respect to substantially identical transactions."

[91] *Farmland Indus. v. Commissioner,* 78 T.C.M. (CCH) 846 (1999); *Illinois Grain Corp. v. Commissioner,* 87 T.C. 435, 459 (1986); Rev. Rul. 75-228, 1975-1 C.B. 278.

with its patrons, and which benefits the patrons other than incidentally through the generation of extra income, is business 'with or for' patrons."[92] The determination as to whether cooperative income is patronage-sourced largely depends of the specific facts of the cooperative enterprise and the way that the cooperative conducts its business.[93]

The directly related/actually facilitates test includes some certain common cooperative business activities. For instance, cooperative activity in negotiating and administering supply contracts with third parties on behalf of their patrons clearly generate patronage-sourced income even though the cooperative doesn't do business directly with the patrons. Similarly, cooperative purchases of ingredients or other products that are combined with or incorporated into their patron's products for marketing purposes also generate patronage-sourced income.[94]

The directly related/actually facilitates test also encompasses activities more remote from the cooperative's core mission. Capital gains received by a cooperative from the sale of assets used in its business or equity investments in businesses which assisted the cooperative's activities have been held to be patronage-sourced. In *St. Louis Bank*, for instance, the court held that interest income earned by a cooperative bank on surplus income was patronage-sourced income because such income reduced the cost of loanable funds and thereby "lessen[ed] costs for the credit provided to its patrons." Similarly, in *Land O'Lakes, Inc. v. U.S.*, the court held that dividends

---

[92] *St. Louis Bank for Cooperatives v. United States*, 624 F.2d 1041, 1051-52 (Ct. Cl. 1980).

[93] *Illinois Grain Corp.*, 87 T.C. at 463.

[94] The conclusion that ingredients or complementary products generate patronage-sourced income only comes into question when such ingredients are greater in value or quantity than the patrons' products.

paid to a cooperative on the stock of a cooperative bank constituted patronage-sourced income because the co-operative was required to acquire the stock to obtain a loan from the cooperative bank, and the terms of the loan were more favorable than market terms.[95] Because the acquisition of the stock "actually facilitated the coop-erative's activities by providing financing on terms favor-able to the cooperative," the dividend income from the stock was "from a patronage source and therefore was properly deductible as a patronage dividend."[96] In *Cotter & Co. v. U.S.*,[97] the court held that a hardware supply co-operative's interest income from short-term commercial paper was patronage-sourced where the cooperative needed to maintain significant liquidity to run its business and proper financial management practices dictated that excess funds should be invested in interest-bearing secu-rities.[98]

The determination of whether a particular type of coop-erative activity generates patronage-sourced income de-pends on the specific facts of that activity and can be quite complex. Cooperatives should consider consulting an experienced cooperative attorney if uncertainty exists about a specific activity.

(iii)   Based on Patronage

Finally, a patronage dividend must be paid to patrons based on the "quantity" or "value" of each patron's busi-ness with the cooperative.[99] The choice of calculating pat-ronage according to "quantity" or "value" gives a coop-erative considerable flexibility in calculating patronage

---

[95] *Land O'Lakes, Inc. v. U.S.*, 675 F.2d 988 (8th Cir. 1982).

[96] *Id.* at 993.

[97] *Cotter & Co. v. U.S.*, 765 F.2d 1102 (Fed. Cir. 1985).

[98] *Accord Illinois Grain Corp.*, 87 T.C. at 459-61.

[99] I.R.C. § 1388(a). *See also* CAL. CORP. CODE § 12201.

dividends. Under this rule, cooperatives can calculate and distribute proportionately greater patronage dividends to patrons whose transactions are more valuable or profitable to the cooperative. Cooperatives should consult with an experienced cooperative attorney if they have questions about potential ways of calculating patronage.

A special rule for calculating patronage applies to patronage-sourced cooperative income from the sale of assets or investments. The rule is that the cooperative should allocate such gain, "insofar as practicable," to those persons who were patrons during the holding period of the asset and in accordance with their patronage during such period. [100] Deviations from this rule are permitted on grounds of practicality, and thus the IRS has specifically held that a cooperative allocating patronage-sourced capital gain need not make allocations to non-members, former members or dead members on grounds that it would be too difficult to locate the excluded classes.[101]

(iv)   Distributions that Fail to Qualify as Patronage Dividends

As noted above, cooperatives are subject to all the federal tax rules that apply to ordinary C corporations, except insofar as such rules are modified by Subchap-

---

[100] This rule is based on Treas. Reg. § 1.1382-3(c)(3). Though this Regulation by its terms applies only to tax-exempt farmers cooperatives, the IRS has repeatedly applied its principles to all cooperatives for purposes of allocating patronage-sourced capital gains. *See, e.g.*, I.R.S. Priv. Ltr. Rul. 2006-52-003 (Dec. 29, 2006) (Subchapter T cooperative); I.R.S. Priv. Ltr. Rul. 2006-27-007 (July 7, 2006) (Nonexempt Telephone Cooperative); I.R.S. Priv. Ltr. Rul. 2002-52-027 (Dec. 26, 2002) (Subchapter T cooperative); I.R.S. Priv. Ltr. Rul. 2002-39-029 (Sept. 27, 2002) (Nonexempt Telephone Cooperative); I.R.S. Priv. Ltr. Rul. 2001-52-035 (Dec. 28, 2001) (Nonexempt Telephone Cooperative); I.R.S. Priv. Ltr. Rul. 2000-20-031 (May 22, 2000) (Subchapter T cooperative).

[101] I.R.S. Priv. Ltr. Rul. 2009-35-019 (Aug. 28, 2009).

ter T or non-statutory cooperative principles. Accordingly, a cooperative distribution which fails to qualify as a patronage dividend is subject to the rules on corporate distributions in Code Section 301 and usually will be treated in whole or part as an ordinary dividend.[102]

(b)   Form of Patronage Dividends

Few cooperatives pay patronage dividends entirely in the form of cash. The Code permits cooperatives to pay deductible patronage dividends in the form of (1) money, (2) "qualified written notices of allocation," and (3) "other property." Most cooperatives pay patronage dividends largely in the form of qualified written notices of allocation.

A qualified written notice of allocation is defined as a written notice of allocation of cooperative equity that meets certain requirements of Subchapter T.[103] The cooperative equity allocated by such notice can take the form of capital stock, capital credits, revolving funds credit, patrons' equities or any other term used by the cooperative's governing documents to describe its equity. Because all cooperative equity must satisfy the subordination of capital requirement, it will always have a stated dollar amount – a face amount that is payable on redemption or liquidation.

To constitute a qualified written notice of allocation, the notice must meet three basic requirements. First, the notice must disclose the stated dollar amount of the allocated cooperative equity and the portion of the same that constitutes a patronage dividend. Second, at least 20% of

---

[102] *See* I.R.C. § 301(c).
[103] I.R.C. § 1388(c)(1).

the patronage dividend of which the allocated cooperative equity is a part must be paid in cash by the cooperative. Third, and most important, the recipient of the notice must have consented to take into income the stated dollar amount of the equity. Most modern cooperatives obtain the necessary consent by including a provision in their bylaws providing that each member so consents, which bylaw provision is sent to each new member. Consent can also be obtained by obtaining a written acknowledgment or by issuing and having the recipient cash a check which provides that cashing constitutes consent (a "qualified check"). As further discussed below, the stated amount of a qualified written notice of allocation is deductible by the cooperative even if such amount greatly exceeds the fair market value of such notice.

Though cooperatives can also pay patronage dividends in the form of "other property," they rarely do so. For this purpose, "other property is defined by Subchapter T to exclude the cooperative's own equity.[104] Most patronage dividend distributions of "other property" consist of equity interests in other business entities in which the cooperative has an interest.

(c) Payment Period for Patronage Dividends

In order to deduct a patronage dividend from income for a taxable year, a cooperative must pay the patronage dividend during the "payment period" for the taxable year.[105] Subchapter T defines the payment period as beginning on the first day of the taxable year and ending on the

---

[104] Distributions of cooperative equity either fall within the category of qualified written notices of allocation or fall outside it, in which case such distributions constitute "nonqualified written notices of allocation," which are expressly excluded from the definition of other property. *See* I.R.C. §§ 1382(b), 1388(d).

[105] I.R.C. § 1382(b).

fifteenth day of the ninth month following the close of such taxable year.[106] Two observations should be made. First, a cooperative can pay patronage dividends during the taxable year to which they relate. Because patronage dividends must be calculated based on net income, however, such mid-year patronage dividends must be estimated and an additional round of patronage dividends will generally have to be distributed after actual net income is calculated. Second, a cooperative does not have to pay patronage dividends until 8-½ months after the close of its taxable year, for example, by September 15 if its taxable year ends on December 31. This 8-½ month period ends on the same date in which the cooperative's federal income tax is due (including all extensions) and gives the cooperative time to calculate its net income for the year.

(d)   Tax Consequences of Patronage Dividends

For the cooperative, patronage dividends calculated and paid in conformity with the requirements of Subchapter T can be deducted from the cooperative's net income.[107] The effect of this deduction is that the cooperative can eliminate all of its patronage-sourced income, which accordingly will not be subject to federal income tax at the cooperative level. All non-patronage-sourced income (and all patronage-sourced income not paid as patronage dividends or another deductible cooperative distribution) is subject to federal corporate income tax.

For the patron, patronage dividends generally must be included in income in the taxable year of receipt, which

---

[106] I.R.C. § 1382(d).
[107] I.R.C. § 1382(b).

is often the taxable year following that in which the co-operative deducted the amount.[108] Two exceptions to the rule of inclusion exist.[109] First, patronage dividends are not includable in income if they result from transactions involving "personal, living or family items," such as purchases of food or clothing. Second, patronage dividends are not includable in income if they arise as a result of the purchase of depreciable property and are properly treated as an adjustment to the tax basis of the property. Both exceptions reflect the theory that patronage dividends are theoretically purchase price adjustments.[110] In the case of personal property, the purchase price of such items has been reduced and no addition to income is necessary because the original price was never deducted as a business expense. In the case of depreciable property, the purchase price of such property has been reduced and the purchaser should account for this by lowering the tax basis subject to depreciation.

The amount of a patronage dividend includible in the patron's income is equal to the cash, stated dollar amount of qualified written notices of allocation, and fair market value of other property received in the distribution. Such amount constitutes ordinary income (even if some of it arose from capital gain of the cooperative) and is generally subject to the self-employment tax imposed by Section 1401 of the Code, if received by an individual.[111]

A patron who receives cooperative equity in a qualified written notice of allocation will have a tax basis in such

---

[108] I.R.C. § 1385(a).

[109] I.R.C. § 1385(b).

[110] *See* Treas. Reg. § 1.61-5(b)(3)(i) (explaining the justification for these exceptions, which predate the enactment of Subchapter T).

[111] *Shumaker v. Commissioner*, 648 F.2d 1198, 1200 (9th Cir. 1981)

equity equal to its stated dollar amount. Accordingly, redemption of such equity at its stated dollar amount by the cooperative will not give rise to any taxable income.

Section 2.4 Limited Cooperative Act ("LCA") Taxation

LCAs are treated like partnerships for federal tax purposes. The members themselves are taxed as they would be in a partnership, and the institution is not taxed at that level.[112] That means that LCAs are full pass-through entities, as compared to the partial pass-through entity of cooperatives under Subchapter T. LCAs file informational returns in the states in which they do business, and members may need to file returns in those states. LCAs should consult tax counsel on return filing and taxation issues.

---

[112] *See also*, Section 2.2.

CHAPTER III
BOARD OF DIRECTORS

Section 3.1   Introduction

Cooperatives can be organized under the cooperative law of any state or under the general corporation statute of any state. Many state cooperatives laws apply the general corporation statute of the state to cooperatives if it is not inconsistent with the more specific state cooperatives law.[113] For example, the Minnesota Cooperatives Law provides that the Minnesota Business Corporations Act applies to cooperatives if its provisions do not contradict the express provisions of the Cooperatives Law.[114] Similarly, three different incorporation statutes in Washington apply to cooperatives. The Business Corporation Act applies to cooperatives, unless those provisions conflict with, or inconsistent with, the express provisions of the Cooperative Associations statute.[115] Such overlapping statutory schemes exist in various jurisdictions and can create confusion and legal ambiguities.[116] Since many provisions of the applicable statutes allow cooperatives to self-regulate certain matters through the cooperative's bylaws, it is good practice to use such bylaws to pre-empt, eliminate, or clarify ambiguities.

---

[113] A summary of the jurisdictions with specific statutes governing cooperatives is contained in the Appendix.

[114] *See* MINN. STAT. ANN. § 308A.201 subdiv. 1(2).

[115] *See* WASH. REV. CODE § 23.86.360; *see also*, WASH. REV. CODE § 24.06, *et seq.*

[116] *See* note following WASH. REV. CODE § 23.86.007 (Legislative finding – 1989 c 307).

Section 3.2   Selection

(a)   General Requirements

Different jurisdictions set minimum requirements for the number of board members. For example, under Washington law, a cooperative must be governed by a board of three or more directors, whereas Minnesota law requires five members.[117] Boards of directors are important because a cooperative can only act by or under the authority of the board.[118] Generally speaking, "business and affairs of [any] corporation shall be managed under the direction of its board of directors, which shall have exclusive authority as to substantive decisions concerning management of the corporation's business."[119] As discussed in other chapters, for tax and antitrust reasons many agricultural cooperatives operate on a one member, one vote principle.[120] Members of the cooperative elect the directors, and the cooperative's bylaws may prescribe the time, place, and procedure for electing the directors. Once elected, a director holds office during the term for which they were elected and until their successors are elected and qualified.[121]

---

[117] *Compare* WASH. REV. CODE § 23.86.080, *with* MINN. STAT. ANN. § 308A.301 (requiring cooperatives to have at least five directors on the board, except cooperative housing corporations, which must have at least three directors). *See also* CAL. CORP. CODE § 12331(a) (requiring a minimum of three directors); OR. REV. STAT. § 62.280(4) (requiring a minimum of three directors, unless the number of cooperative members is less than three, in which case the number of directors must equal the number of members); WIS. STAT. § 185.31 (requiring a minimum of five directors, or if the cooperative has less than fifty members, a minimum of three directors).

[118] *See* CAL. CORP. CODE § 12350; MINN. STAT. ANN. § 308A.301; OR. REV. STAT. § 62.280(1); WASH. REV. CODE § 23B.08.010; WIS. STAT. § 185.31(1).

[119] WASH. REV. CODE § 23B.080.010(b); CAL. CORP. CODE § 12350.

[120] *See* CAL. CORP. CODE § 12404; MINN. STAT. ANN. § 308A.635 subdiv. 1; OR. REV. STAT. § 62.265(1); WASH. REV. CODE § 23.86.115; WIS. STAT. § 185.52(1)(a).

[121] *See* CAL. CORP. CODE § 12360(b); MINN. STAT. ANN. § 308A.311 subdiv. 1; OR. REV. STAT. § 62.280(5); WASH. REV. CODE § 23.86.080(1); WIS. STAT.

(b)   Vacancies on the Board of Directors

State cooperatives statutes generally state that any vacancy that occurs on the board of directors, including vacancies that arise because of an increase in the number of directors, can be filled by the board of directors unless the cooperative's articles of incorporation or bylaws prescribe a different method for filling such vacancies.[122] A director elected or appointed to fill a vacancy is elected or appointed for the unexpired term of the predecessor in office.[123] Under the Minnesota Cooperatives Law, for example, the board may appoint a member of the cooperative to fill a vacant board position until the next regular or special members' meeting, at which the members must elect a director to fill the unexpired term of the vacant director's position.[124]

If the vacancy was due to the director's removal through a special removal procedure (which is described later on in this chapter), the vacancy should be filled with the procedure required by the removal statute.[125] Under the Washington Business Corporation Act, for example, unless the articles of incorporation specify otherwise, a vacancy that occurs on a board of directors, including a vacancy resulting from an increase in the number of directors, can be filled by the following:[126]

- The shareholders;

- The board of directors; or

---

§ 185.31(3).

[122] *See* CAL. CORP. CODE § 12364(a); MINN. STAT. ANN. § 308A.315; OR. REV. STAT. § 62.280(7); WASH. REV. CODE § 23.86.080(2); WIS. STAT. § 185.31(5).

[123] *See* CAL. CORP. CODE § 12360(b); MINN. STAT. ANN. § 308A.315; OR. REV. STAT. § 62.280(7); WASH. REV. CODE § 23.86.080(2); WIS. STAT. § 185.31(5).

[124] MINN. STAT. ANN. § 308A.315.

[125] *See* WASH. REV. CODE § 23.86.087.

[126] *See* WASH. REV. CODE § 23B.08.100.

- If the directors in office constitute less than a quorum of the board, they may fill the vacancy by the affirmative vote of a majority of all the directors in office.[127]

There are additional requirements in the following circumstances:

- If the vacant office was held by a director elected by a voting group of shareholders, only the holders of shares of that voting group are entitled to vote to fill the vacancy, if it is filled by the shareholders, and only the directors elected by that voting group are entitled to fill the vacancy if it is filled by the directors.[128]

- A vacancy that will occur at a specific later date, by reason of a resignation effective at a later date or otherwise, may be filled before the vacancy occurs, but the new director may not take office until the vacancy occurs.[129]

- If the articles of incorporation authorize dividing the shares into classes or series, the articles may also authorize the election of all or a specified number of directors by the holders of one or more authorized classes or series of shares. A class, or classes, or series of shares entitled to elect one or more directors, is a separate voting group for purposes of the election of directors.[130]

Both Washington statutes condition certain requirements on the absence of contrary articles of

---

[127] WASH. REV. CODE § 23B.08.100(1), *see also* WASH. REV. CODE § 23.86.125 (quorum).

[128] WASH. REV. CODE § 23B.08.100(2).

[129] WASH. REV. CODE § 23B.08.100(3).

[130] WASH. REV. CODE § 23B.08.040.

incorporation or bylaws. Due to the potential for ambiguity and confusion, it is advisable for a cooperative to expressly specify procedures for filling vacancies through its bylaws.

Washington law further allows cooperatives to institute supplemental requirements for selection of its board of directors. For example, a cooperative, through its bylaws, can specify which qualifications a director must possess, or require directors to be residents of Washington, shareholders of the cooperative, or both. Absent such a directive, a director need not be a state resident or a shareholder of the corporation under state law.[131]

PRACTICAL TIP

Boards that are too small may be difficult to schedule in order to get a quorum (majority) available to be present, while boards that are too large may be difficult to manage. While there is no magic number, many cooperative boards have about 10 members, each with staggered three year terms to encourage continuity and avoid wholesale replacement.

Section 3.3   Removal

Jurisdictions address the removal of directors in different ways.[132] The Minnesota Cooperatives Law, for example, simply provides that the members of a cooperative may remove a director for cause related to the director's duties.[133]

---

[131] WASH. REV. CODE § 23B.08.020.
[132] *See, e.g.,* CAL. CORP. CODE §§ 12362-12363; MINN. STAT. ANN. § 308A.321; OR. REV. STAT. § 62.280(6); WASH. REV. CODE § 23.86.087; WIS. STAT. § 185.31(4).
[133] MINN. STAT. ANN. § 308A.321.

In California, removal can vary based on the cooperative's size. If there are less than 50 members, removal must be approved by a majority of all members (all votes entitled to be cast)[134]; or for cooperatives with more than 50 members, a majority vote of members.[135] California law strictly limits a board's ability to remove members otherwise.[136] The Board may declare a position vacant (effectively removing the director), if the director's eligibility for election as a director has ceased, or has been declared of unsound mind by a final order of court, or convicted of a felony, or, if at the time a director is elected, the bylaws provide that a director may be removed for missing a specified number of board meetings, fails to attend the specified number of meetings.[137] Directors may be removed by lawsuit (called "judicial proceedings" in the statute).[138]

Washington's Cooperative Associations statute, on the other hand, lists steps by which any member of a cooperative may bring charges against a director of the cooperative:[139]

- First, a member must file charges in writing with the secretary of the association, together with a petition signed by ten percent of the members requesting the removal of the director in question.

- The removal shall be voted upon at the next regular or special meeting of the association and, by a vote of a majority of the members voting, the

---

[134] CAL. CORP. CODE § 12362(a), 12223.

[135] CAL. CORP. CODE § 12362(a).

[136] CAL. CORP. CODE § 12362(e), cross-referencing §§ 12361 (vacancy) and 12363 (judicial removal).

[137] CAL. CORP. CODE § 12361.

[138] CAL. CORP. CODE § 12363.

[139] *See* WASH. REV. CODE § 23.86.087.

association may remove the officer or director and fill the vacancy. The director against whom such charges have been brought shall be informed in writing of the charges prior to the meeting and shall have an opportunity at the meeting to be heard in person, or by counsel, and to present witnesses. The person or persons bringing the charges shall have the same opportunity.

- If the bylaws provide for election of directors by districts, the petition for removal of a director must be signed by the number of members residing in the district from which the officer or director was elected as the articles of incorporation or bylaws specify, and, in the absence of such specification, the petition must be signed by ten percent of the members residing in the district. The board of directors must call a special meeting of the members residing in that district to consider the removal of the director. By a vote of the majority of the members of the district voting, the association may remove the officer or director and fill the vacancy.

In contrast to the above, the removal process under the Washington Business Corporation Act is divided into two kinds,[140] namely: (i) removal of directors by shareholders and (ii) removal of directors by judicial proceeding. The procedure for each is discussed below:

- Removal of Directors by Shareholders.[141]

  o Shareholders of a corporation may remove one or more directors with or without cause

---

[140] *See* WASH. REV. CODE § 23B.08.080-.090.
[141] *See* WASH. REV. CODE § 23B.08.080(1-4).

unless the articles of incorporation provide that directors may be removed only for cause.

o If a director is elected by holders of one or more authorized classes or series of shares, only the holders of those classes or series of shares may participate in the vote to remove the director.

o If cumulative voting is authorized, and if less than the entire board is to be removed, no director may be removed if the number of votes sufficient to elect the director under cumulative voting is voted against the director's removal. If cumulative voting is not authorized, a director may be removed only if the number of votes cast to remove the director exceeds the number of votes cast not to remove the director (*i.e.*, a simple majority).[142]

o A director may be removed by the shareholders only at a special meeting called for the purpose of removing the director, and the meeting notice must state that the purpose, or one of the purposes, of the meeting is removal of the director.

- Removal of Directors by Judicial Proceeding.[143]

o The superior court of the county where a corporation's principal office or, if none in this state, its registered office is located may remove a director of the corporation from office in a proceeding commenced either by

---

[142] WASH. REV. CODE § 23B.08.080.

[143] *See* WASH. REV. CODE § 23B.08.090. The California cooperatives statute also provides for judicial removal of directors. CAL. CORP. CODE § 12363.

the corporation or by its shareholders holding at least ten percent of the outstanding
shares of any class if the court finds that:

- The director engaged in fraudulent or
  dishonest conduct with respect to the
  corporation.

- Removal is in the best interest of the corporation.

o The court that removes a director may bar
  the director from reelection for a period prescribed by the court.

o If shareholders commence a proceeding under subsection (1) of this section, they shall
  make the corporation a party defendant.

As evident from a comparison of the two statutes above,
the Washington Business Corporation Act provides for
judicial removal while the Washington Cooperative Associations statute does not. It is unclear whether the
Washington Business Corporation Act provisions for judicial removal allow for such removal of cooperative
board members. In a case involving a non-profit cooperation and similar differences in statutory provisions, a
Washington appellate court ruled that the judicial removal provisions of the Washington Business Corporations Act, did not apply to non-profit corporations, in
light of the existence of a statute for non-profits which
did not contain the judicial removal provision.[144] That
reasoning has been rendered moot, with the passage of a

---

[144] *See Lyzanchuk v. Yakima Ranches Owners Ass'n*, 73 Wn. App. 1, 6-7 (1994).

subsequent, superseding statute that expressly grants judicial removal for non-profit corporations.[145] The issue however, is not settled in the context of cooperatives, which is why it is good practice to pre-empt and resolve such ambiguities through express provisions in the cooperative's bylaws.

> ### PRACTICAL TIP
>
> *It is very hard to remove directors after they have been approved by the members or appointed by the board. There are good policy reasons for this, as it promotes democratic control and supports the member vote. Problems can be avoided by employing several strategies:*
>
> 1. *Select well by using nominating committees and pre-nomination vetting, required before consideration as a board member.*
> 2. *Set director specific qualifications. Some jurisdictions permit the board to declare a member no longer qualified, effectively removing them.*
> 3. *Require attendance at a specific number of meetings per year.*
> 4. *Engage an outside firm to prepare a performance review for each board member, and report to the Board Chair.*

Section 3.4   Director Duties

Members of the board of directors of cooperatives are subject to the same responsibilities and duties as the members of the board of directors of corporations in

---

[145] *See* WASH. REV. CODE § 24.03.1031; *see also Kidisti Sekkassue Orthodox Tewehado Eritrean Church v. Medin*, 118 Wn. App. 1022 (2003) (discussing the superseding statute).

general. Additionally, the members of the board of directors of cooperatives have duties that are unique to cooperatives, due to the special relationship between directors and members of cooperatives. Directors must balance the conflicting interests and needs of the members of the cooperative. In making decisions, directors should not confine themselves to considerations of what is profitable, but must also consider the needs of their individual members.

Sometimes, decisions that may be appropriate for general corporations might not be appropriate in the cooperative setting, and directors of cooperatives must be mindful of that distinction.[146] State laws may specify the general duties that members of boards of directors must perform, in the absence of bylaws or statutory limitations.[147] Some state statutes expressly permit the cooperative to specify the powers and duties of the directors in the bylaws.[148] Considering the variety that exists among different cooperatives, it is advisable for a cooperative to shape the duties and responsibilities of its board of directors through its bylaws, so as to effectively address a particular cooperative's specific needs.

The duties of the board of directors of cooperatives can be divided into the following three main aspects: responsibilities, standards of conduct, and liabilities. Responsibilities describe what the board must do to meet its obligations to the cooperative under laws and other guiding sources. Standards of conduct describe how the

---

[146] *See* James Baarda, Co-op Boards' Circle of Responsibilities, Cooperative Information Report 3 (Feb. 2003), *available at*: www.rurdev.usda.gov/rbs/pub/cir61.pdf.

[147] *See generally* WASH. REV. CODE § 23B.08.010; MINN. STAT. ANN. § 302A.201 subdiv. 1.

[148] *See, e.g.*, CAL. CORP. CODE § 12331(c)(3); MINN. STAT. ANN. § 308A.165 subdiv. 3; OR. REV. STAT. § 62.280(3); WIS. STAT. § 185.31(1).

responsibilities must be carried out. Liabilities describe the consequences when directors fail to carry out responsibilities or fail to adhere to the standards of conduct, as well as the immunities that the law grants to members of the boards of directors of cooperatives.[149]

(a)   Responsibilities

The responsibilities of a cooperative board of directors member are shaped by both state laws and the cooperative's own bylaws. The cooperative's bylaws provide guidelines intended to effectuate the broad mandate of the state law. As such, there may be differences in responsibilities across different cooperatives based on their bylaws. Board members – especially new ones – should carefully review the cooperative's bylaws and articles to understand the unique duties, if any, that the corporate documents impose on them.

There are a number of basic responsibilities imposed on all members of the board of directors of cooperatives. These include the responsibility to do the following:[150]

- Represent the best interests of cooperative members as a whole.

- Establish the policies of the cooperative.

- Hire and supervise management.

- Ensure sound management of the cooperative.

- Acquire and preserve cooperative assets.

- Preserve the cooperative character of the organization.

---

[149] *See* Baarda, *supra.*
[150] *See id.*

- Assess the cooperative's performance.

- Inform members.

Individual members of the board of directors of a cooperative have the responsibility to do, at a minimum, the following:[151]

- Become familiar with the articles of incorporation and bylaws of the cooperative, and conduct business in accordance with their provisions.

- Attend regular and special meetings of the board.[152]

- Be familiar with the state law under which the cooperative was incorporated.

- Understand the general legal responsibilities of serving on a board of directors.

(b)   Board Member Standards of Conduct

State laws often prescribe the general standards for directors of a cooperative. [153] The standards provide guidance to directors in the discharge of their duties. They also provide guidance to courts, who will generally defer to the decisions made by disinterested[154] and careful members of the board of directors and refuse to "second guess" those decisions.

The relevant subchapter of the Washington Business Corporation Act, for example, states that a director shall

---

[151] U.S. Dep't of Agriculture, Cooperative Information Report 45, Section 6 Understanding Cooperatives: Who Runs the Cooperative Business? (Oct. 1994), *available at*: www.rurdev.usda.gov/rbs/pub/cir456.pdf.

[152] For an example of meeting notice requirements, see CAL. CORP. CODE § 12351.

[153] *See* WASH. REV. CODE § 23B.08.300; MINN. STAT. ANN. § 308A.328.

[154] "Disinterested" refers to the absence of conflicts of interest, a concept discussed below.

discharge the duties of a director, including duties as a member of a committee:

- In good faith.

- With the care an ordinarily prudent person in a like position would exercise under similar circumstances, without the benefit of hindsight.

- In a manner the director reasonably believes to be in the best interests of the corporation.[155]

Similarly, the Minnesota Cooperatives Law requires that a director must discharge the duties of a director:

- In good faith.

- In a manner the director reasonably believes to be in the best interests of the cooperative.

- With the care an ordinary prudent person in a like position would exercise under similar circumstances.[156]

However, directors do not need to act alone. Directors can obtain guidance in making decisions, in the same way they would consult with experts in their own business affairs. For example, a director is entitled to rely on information, opinions, reports, or statements, including financial statements and other financial data, if prepared or presented by officers or employees of the corporation whom the director reasonably believes to be reliable and competent in the matters presented, such as legal counsel, public accountants, other persons as to matters the director reasonably believes are within the person's professional or expert competence, or a committee of the

---

[155] WASH. REV. CODE § 23B.08.300(1).
[156] MINN. STAT. ANN. § 308A.328 subdiv. 1.

board of directors of which the director is not a member if the director reasonably believes the committee merits confidence.[157]

However, directors cannot blindly accept recommendations of others if their own judgment or personal knowledge would instruct otherwise. Many state statutes specifically provide that a director is not acting in good faith if the director has knowledge concerning the matter in question that makes reliance on an outsider or expert unwarranted.[158]

If a director carefully exercises these duties, she or he may be exempted from personal liability for actions or omissions taken.[159]

(c) Liabilities

(i) Immunities Granted to Members of Cooperative Boards of Directors

State statutes often ensure specific immunities from liability for members of a cooperative's board of directors. For example, Washington state law affords directors of cooperatives the following immunities:[160]

- A member of the board of directors of any non-profit corporation (or cooperative) is not individually liable for any discretionary decision

---

[157] *See* CAL. CORP. CODE § 12371(b); MINN. STAT. ANN. § 308A.328 subdiv. 2; OR. REV. STAT. § 62.283(2); WASH. REV. CODE § 23B.08.300(2); WIS. STAT. § 185.363.

[158] *See, e.g.*, CAL. CORP. CODE § 12371(b)(3); MINN. STAT. ANN. § 308A.328 subdiv. 2(b); OR. REV. STAT. § 62.283(3); WASH. REV. CODE § 23B.08.300(3); WIS. STAT. § 185.363.

[159] *See, e.g.*, CAL. CORP. CODE § 12371(c); MINN. STAT. ANN. § 308A.328 subdiv. 1; OR. REV. STAT. § 62.283(4); WASH. REV. CODE § 23B.08.300(4); WIS. STAT. § 185.367(1).

[160] *See* WASH. REV. CODE § 4.24.264; *see also* WASH. REV. CODE § 23.86.030(3).

or failure to make a discretionary decision within his or her official capacity as director or officer unless the decision or failure to decide constitutes gross negligence.[161] This immunity does not however, limit or modify in any manner, the duties or liabilities of a director of a cooperative to the cooperative association or the cooperative's members.[162]

- In addition, the Cooperative Associations statute requires cooperative associations formed under the cooperative statute after 1989 to prepare articles of incorporation in writing which will specify any lawful provision which the incorporators elect to put in place to regulate the internal affairs of the association. Such provisions may include:[163]

  o Provisions eliminating or limiting the personal liability of a director to the association or its members for monetary damages for conduct as a director, provided that such a provision does *not* eliminate or limit the liability of a director for the following:

    - Acts or omissions that involve intentional misconduct by a director; or

    - A knowing violation of law by a director; or

    - Any transaction from which the director will personally receive a benefit in

---

[161] *See* WASH. REV. CODE § 4.24.264(1); *see also* WASH. REV. CODE § 23.86.050(12)(a) (exclusion must be contained in the articles of incorporation).

[162] *See* WASH. REV. CODE § 4.24.264(2).

[163] *See* WASH. REV. CODE § 23.86.050(12); *see also* MINN. STAT. ANN. § 308A.325 (providing similar restrictions on the ability to limit liability in the articles).

money, property, or services to which the
director is not legally entitled.

Importantly, such provisions cannot retroactively eliminate or limit the liability of a director for any actions or
omissions occurring before the date when such provision
becomes effective. However, the board could ratify decisions made earlier, and/or indemnify the directions for
their actions if permitted by law.

(ii)   Conflicts of Interest

Directors must avoid conflicts of interest. A conflict of
interest transaction is one with the corporation in which
a member of the board of directors of a cooperative has
a direct or indirect interest.[164] A conflict of interest transaction is not voidable by the corporation solely because
of the director's interest.[165] Conflict of interest problems
can be exacerbated due to the nature of cooperatives,
where by definition board members are customers of the
cooperative.

There are actions, however, that directors can take to ensure compliance with the rules regarding conflict of interest transactions. Board members with a direct conflict
of interest should disclose the nature of the conflict to
the other directors and, in many cases, should recuse
themselves from discussion and voting on matters where
they have a direct interest in the underlying transaction.
When a conflict exists, all of the board members should
be careful to satisfy the duty of diligence, duty of loyalty,
and duty of care. General guidelines on the duties of directors are found in state corporation or cooperatives
laws and are discussed below. Following the standard of

---

[164] *See id.*
[165] *See* CAL. CORP. CODE § 12373; MINN. STAT. ANN. § 302A.255 subdiv. 1; OR.
REV. STAT. § 62.284; WASH. REV. CODE § 23B.08.700-.720.

care provisions of these statutes – in other words, exercising sound business judgment – substantially lessens the likelihood of being successfully challenged on conflict of interest violations.

PRACTICAL TIP

Cooperative board members are also members – they use the cooperative's products and services. As such, there is always a mild conflict involved in decision-making. For example, board members will benefit if prices are reduced.

These conflicts will not always create legal exposure. However, board members should be wary of issues they are deciding where they will receive a disproportionate benefit. For example, volume rebates would disproportionately benefit larger users, who might also be board members. These conflicts are best resolved by acknowledging them when they arise, making decisions that benefit all members, and where necessary asking the board member with the conflict to refrain from voting (called "recusal").

(iii) Duties of Diligence, Loyalty and Care

Duty of diligence (sometimes called duty of attention), refers to the need for directors to stay informed, and participate actively in the affairs of the cooperative. This keeps them abreast with current events as far as the cooperative is concerned and minimizes errors due to oversight.

Duty of loyalty is the acknowledgment that directors are in a position of trust with the cooperative, and must not abuse the relationship for their personal enrichment. This can be challenging in the cooperative context where some dealing between a director and the cooperative, tends to be inevitable.

Duty of care refers to the duty to act in good faith, and in the best interest of the cooperative. The director must act as a prudent person would on their own business, under similar circumstances. It is a standard that allows taking risks, as long as they are reasonable under the circumstances. A director, under this standard, need not guarantee the result of his or her decision, but that it was arrived at honestly and prudently. The business judgment rule, discussed below, is related to the duty of care standard.

> ### PRACTICAL TIP
> *Cooperative board members are often members of other co-ops. Board members frequently sit on other boards. This can create issues of duty of loyalty and self-dealing. Board members should disclose whenever they are addressing another co-op or entity in which they have a membership or financial interest.*

(iv)   Business Judgment Rule

The decisions of directors can be highly susceptible to hindsight criticisms. In response, courts have developed the doctrine called the business judgment rule.

In a nutshell, the business judgment rule is the doctrine that directors of a commercial corporation may take chances, as a prudent man would in his own business. The court will not hold directors liable for honest errors, or mistakes of judgment, as long as they act in good faith.[166]

> ### PRACTICAL TIP
>
> *Being selected by other members– often competitors or respected business people – to represent them is quite an honor! Once on the Board, however, your duties change. You now represent the entire organization. Not just the constituency that voted for you. The honor of being on the Board carries with it duties to the cooperative and its members that are more important legally than the board member's role as a member, friend or family member. Suddenly, issues like confidentiality, conflicts of interest, and accountability become critical. Board members should be required to participate in training to emphasize their new role and the importance of legal compliance.*

Section 3.5   Confidentiality

While usually there are no specific state statutes governing confidentiality among cooperatives, directors must still exercise care and diligence when it comes to disseminating and sharing information. In other words, they must act in accordance with the cooperative's procedures, policies and bylaws, and as a reasonably prudent person. Directors must exercise circumspection in the following non-exhaustive areas and scenarios:

- When divulging information or publication will jeopardize the cooperative, or put it at a competitive disadvantage.

---

[166] *See Para-Medical Leasing v. Hangen,* 48 Wn. App. 389, 394 (1987).

- Personnel matters.

- Real estate acquisitions.

- Business acquisitions and partnerships.

- Lease negotiations.

- Litigation.

The above areas are common but by no means exhaustive. It is strongly recommended as a good risk mitigation practice to have a signed board code of ethics prohibiting activities that breach confidentiality.[167]

Many cooperatives have policies limiting the right of directors to discuss Board deliberations with cooperative members and others. The purpose of such a policy is to ensure that deliberations are open and robust and decisions are made with deliberation and a view toward the best interest of the members rather than for political reasons. Cooperative boards also often decide it is best practice for all directors to use the same message when explaining controversial decisions made by the directors. It is often good practice for directors to discuss these matters when controversial or very important decisions are made.

Section 3.6   Special Role With Members

Cooperatives are created and operated to serve the needs of their members, who are both owners and users of the cooperative, as distinguished from normal corporations.[168] The board of directors is the governing body that

---

[167] A sample confidentiality policy is attached as Appendix D. *See also* John Corbett & Karen Zimbelman, *Confidentiality: An Issue for Co-op Boards*, Coop. Grocer Network (Dec. 14, 1988), *available at*: www.cooperativegrocer.coop/articles/2004-01-09/confidentiality-issue-co-op-boards.

[168] Understanding Cooperatives: Who Runs the Cooperative Business?, *supra*.

oversees management of the cooperative and thus addresses the needs and desires of individual members.[169] Consequently, an important aspect of the functions of the board of directors is the effective representation of the best interests of the members of the cooperative, as a whole. In representing the members' interests, the board must recognize and balance competing interests at the individual level, both among individual members, and between an individual and the cooperative as a whole. In order to do this effectively, the board must first know the needs of its members. (An exception to this duty occurs when a cooperative is insolvent; in this case, the board's duty shifts to the best interests of the creditors.)

Communication is an important aspect of the relationship between the board of directors of a cooperative and its members. Communication in the context of cooperatives is two-fold. The board must, on the one hand, listen to the concerns of its members, and on the other, inform the members of the cooperative's position and policies. Communicating and informing requires a careful balance between maintaining confidentiality (as discussed above) and transparency. This requires, at a minimum, ensuring that there are mechanisms for member input,[170] and making regular reports to members.[171]

The board members must also familiarize themselves with the rights of members as prescribed by state and federal laws, and the cooperative's own bylaws.

---

[169] *See* Baarda, *supra*.

[170] *See* California Center for Cooperative Development ("CCCD"), *Basic Responsibilities of The Co-Op Board of Directors*, *available at*: www.cccd.coop/files/Board%20 Roles%20&%20Resp.pdf.

[171] *Id.*

PRACTICAL TIP

Everyone has difficulty keeping secrets, especially from their friends and family members. Many cooperatives operate in small business communities, where rumors can run quickly. It is very difficult to maintain confidentiality of business opportunities and board deliberations. But remember – loose lips sink ships! Board members should be cautioned to avoid discussing confidential matters with members or outside the board room. Even comments that are overheard at the local café can create difficult situations for the cooperative, limit business opportunities, and create legal risk for the board members involved.

CHAPTER IV
MEMBERS, OFFICERS, MANAGEMENT, AND RELATION TO THE BOARD

Section 4.1 Introduction

Cooperative members can include individuals, companies, groups, farms, and even other cooperatives. An essential element of the cooperative business form is that the membership uses the products and services of the cooperative. Members therefore have a direct interest in ensuring effective management of the cooperative's affairs.

Section 4.2 Officers and Management

Cooperative board members are users of the cooperative's services as customers or producers (or suppliers). They run their own business and, as with other corporate forms, should focus primary effort towards setting strategic vision, hiring a key executive such as CEO or General Manager, then supervising the efforts and outcome of that individual.[172]

Section 4.3 Duties: Board or CEO?

There is often a natural tension between the board and CEO. This is a struggle for cooperatives in particular. As

---

[172] *See* CAL. CORP. CODE § 12353.

members and service users, cooperative board members have multiple contacts and relationships with the cooperative.[173] The board often sets boundaries in the executive's employment agreement and its own policies. In many practical respects, however, decisions require a collaborative effort between the board and the CEO. The following examples demonstrate that collaboration.

As a starting place, the law makes clear that ultimate accountability to members is vested in the board of directors.[174] The board may grant certain authority to officers, agents, and employees as permitted under the cooperative's articles, bylaws, and applicable laws. The CEO in turn, is accountable to the board and initiates action within the boundaries of authority granted by the board.

While the board of directors is primarily concerned with strategic decisions and internal governance processes, the cooperative's executives are primarily concerned with action and tactical decisions. Decisions on overall objectives, policies and goals of the cooperative are the responsibility of the Board. Decisions related to attaining objectives and goals are the responsibility of the executives.

Decisions involving long range and consequential commitment of resources, such as purchase or upgrade of facilities, finances, or manpower, are the board's responsibility, although usually made with input and recommendations from the executives. Decisions involving intermediate and short-range commitment of resources, and the organization and control of these resources, are the responsibility of executives, although

---

[173] *See*, Chapters III and IV.
[174] A sample position description for board members is attached as Appendix C.

made consistent with budgets and strategies established by Board.

The board should ensure effective succession planning for key executives by providing for executive depth and training, in collaboration with executive management.

Board member recruitment, selection, training, and performance are responsibilities of the board chairperson and other board members (or, often, a governance committee).

Evaluation of the executive and board performance, decisions involving long range and substantial financial commitments and financial structure, objectives and policies, and public and shareholder relations are the board's responsibility. However, operations and subordinate managers and employees oversight, including decisions involving management of budgets, procurement, production, and marketing plans, and industrial/employee relations programs are the responsibility of the executives.[175]

---

[175] As discussed in more detail in Section 8.4 below, board members should usually avoid giving direct instructions or feedback to non-executives of the cooperative, otherwise, executive authority is diminished. While true for other corporate forms, this requires more restraint for cooperative board members due to their multifaceted relationship with the cooperative and its employees.

> ### PRACTICAL TIP
>
> *Cooperative board members are customers, owners, and board members. This often creates a tension with management. Some cooperative boards are inclined to defer to management on all things. However, the board reports to and has duties to members, not management. Board members should observe, ask questions, and hold management accountable to run the operation in an efficient manner that meets the members' objectives.*

Section 4.4   Roles and Responsibilities Compared to the Board

The board does not engage in the operation or day-to-day management of the company. By delegating and approving management programs and actions, the board plans and controls the overall course and performance of the cooperative. The board can replace the CEO if it believes performance is unsatisfactory: however, the board must not supplant management by trying to do management's job itself. Decisions can be made solely by the board, made by management, or shared by both. Examples of the types of decisions that may be made solely by the board, and those made solely by the CEO, or shared by both, are as follows:

Board Decisions Solely:

- Defining long term objectives of the cooperative, including setting policies, and goals (however, with management participation and recommendations).

- Electing board and corporate officers including the chair, vice chair, secretary, and treasurer.

- Making or approving any long-term financial commitments including sources and types of financing with management input.

- Selection of CEO and setting her/his salary. Defining duties of the CEO, and overseeing the CEO's performance.

- Employing an independent auditing firm.

- Retaining board legal counsel (if considered necessary).

- Filling board position vacancies.

- Make basic changes in financial structure with management input.

- Approval of major plans and commitments.

- Matters where member approvals are required, such as amending articles or bylaws, mergers, or sale of substantially all the business assets.

- Approval of the employee retirement and retention program(s).

Management Decisions Primarily:[176]

- Basic ongoing relationships with key providers, including suppliers, vendors, customers and day-to-day relationships with the cooperative's members.

---

[176] Note that these are primary responsibilities of management, which may include consultation with or approval by the board.

- Defining operating or management level objectives, goal s and policies. Short term commitment of resources.

- Preparation of budgets, acquisition and/or disposition plans, and communication of that information to the board.

- Setting manufacturing and/or production plans, establishing asset and marketing plans for approval by the board.

- Defining duties of division managers and department heads.

- Administration of the employee benefits programs, compensation systems, and employee performance evaluation programs consistent with salary scales approved by the board.

- Selection and/or disciplining of employees. Resolution of employee grievances. Measurements of employee performance. Selection of legal counsel for the cooperative.

- Reporting to the board (and members).

- Keeping financial records and preparation and audit of financial reports.

- Compliance with legal requirements.

- Overall management of employee working conditions.

Shared Decision Areas:

- Relations with government, industry and general public.

- Amounts and sources of working capital.

- Engaging selected professional services (*e.g.* legal counsel, consultant) for matters pertaining to joint decision making areas.

- Appraisal of the cooperative's performance.

- Distribution of earnings and development of capitalization and patronage policies.

- Employee bonding.

- Issuing capital instruments.

- Changes in basic organizational structure. Authorizing major facility construction, expansion, etc.

- Capital expenditures exceeding pre-defined CEO authority limits authorized for facility construction, Expansion/replacements.

CHAPTER V
CAPITALIZATION AND FINANCE

Cooperatives, like most other businesses, are generally financed with both debt and equity. Non-cooperative businesses generally allocate their income and assets solely on the basis of the amount of an owner's investments. Similarly, non-cooperative businesses generally grant voting rights to owners in proportion to each owner's investment in the business. Cooperatives, on the other hand, are subject to different requirements, and these requirements have important implications for cooperatives in raising their initial capital, in maintaining sufficient capital on an ongoing basis, and in allocating control and decision making power amongst their owners.

Section 5.1   Cooperative Equity

Cooperatives differ from most businesses because they do business with their owners, who are thus "patrons" of the business. Cooperatives also differ from ordinary corporations because they need to adhere to certain federal tax rules in order to receive "pass through" treatment, which allows them to eliminate some or all of their taxable income (*see* Chapter II). Two of these federal tax rules impose important limitations on cooperative equity. First, the "democratic control" requirement requires cooperatives to limit voting rights to one member, one vote or to allocate voting rights in accordance with patronage.[177] Various state statutes also restrict the voting rights that accompany equity ownership in cooperatives.[178] In accordance with this requirement, cooperative equity instruments generally do not have any voting rights attached to them. At most, a cooperative may issue each member one share of "membership stock" that grants the holder one vote.

Second, the "subordination of capital" requirement requires cooperatives to allocate their income and assets to patrons based on patronage and to give non-patron investors no more than a fixed and limited return on their investment in the cooperative.[179] Based on this requirement, cooperatives cannot issue common stock in the ordinary sense of the term, *i.e.*, an equity instrument that entitles the holder to unlimited dividends and to any appreciation in the value of the business's assets. All cooperative equity rather must have (1) a stated dollar value, sometimes expressed in terms of face amount or par value, which stated value is payable on redemption or liquidation, and (2) a strictly limited right to distributions, generally no more than 8% of stated value.

Cooperative equity generally consists of some or all of the following items:

(a) Membership Stock or Certificates

Some cooperatives require new members to purchase one share of membership stock or a membership certificate for an initial capital investment in the cooperative.

---

[177] *See* Chapter II.
[178] *See, e.g.,* ALASKA STAT. § 10.15.130(a) (bylaws may authorize voting on basis of patronage); CAL. CORP. CODE § 12223; *see also* FLA. STAT. § 618.15(5); N.Y. Coop. Corp. Law § 46.
[179] *Id.*

The initial capital investment is often substantial, and prospective members must pay for the membership stock or certificate over a course of years. The membership share or certificate generally does not entitle the holder to any return other than payment of its face value upon liquidation or termination of membership. Though some cooperatives grant a member voting rights based on ownership of the share or certificate, others base voting rights on membership alone.

(b) Patrons' Equities

Most of the equity in cooperatives takes the form of patrons' equities. Patrons' equities are cooperative equity credits that are paid to members as part of patronage dividends, *i.e.*, cooperative distributions based on patronage which are deductible from the cooperative's income. As noted in Chapter II, cooperatives are permitted under Subchapter T to pay up to 80% of their patronage dividends in the form of cooperative equity. Patrons' equities generally take the form of book entries, are not redeemable at the request of members, and are not entitled to interest or dividends. Cooperatives frequently label their patrons' equities with such names as capital credits, revolving fund credits, patronage equity and the like.

Because patrons' equities are distributed as part of patronage dividends, which are generally paid annually, members of cooperatives increase their equity ownership of the cooperative as they continue to do business with the cooperative. Because patrons' equities generally do not entitle the holder to dividends, holders generally want the cooperative to redeem such patrons' equities as soon as possible. Redemption of patrons' equities is addressed below.

(c)   Preferred Stock

Many cooperatives issue preferred stock as a means of raising additional capital from outside investors as well as members. By issuing preferred stock, cooperatives can raise capital from individuals and organizations that do not necessarily transact business with the cooperative. Generally, this preferred stock carries no voting rights, as decision making power must be confined to patrons on the basis of one-member, one-vote. However, states often require cooperatives to grant preferred shareholders limited voting rights when the value of their shares would be directly affected (*i.e.*, mergers and dissolutions).

While profits can be distributed to preferred shareholders based on the amount invested, distributions are generally limited for federal tax reasons to no more than 8% of the redemption value of the preferred shares.[180] Some states also restrict the maximum distributions that can be made to preferred shareholders.[181] These limitations ensure that cooperatives operate "on a cooperative basis" for the benefit of their patrons and not simply as a profit maximization tool for outside investors. Preferred shareholders also enjoy liquidation preferences should the cooperative be sold or wound up.

Preferred stock offerings are technically an issuance of securities interests in the cooperative. As a result, they must either be issued and registered in a manner compliant with state or federal securities laws, or be subject to

---

[180] I.R.S. Priv. Ltr. Rul. 2011-41-007 (Oct. 14, 2011) (8% dividend is consistent with the subordination of capital requirement); *United Cooperatives, Inc. v. Commissioner*, 4 T.C. 93,106 (1944) (8% dividend is consistent with cooperative operation).

[181] *See, e.g.*, WASH. REV. CODE § 23.86.160; *see also* FLA. STAT. § 618.15(3). Some states such as New York set the limit higher than 8%. *See, e.g.*, N.Y. Coop. Corp. Law § 72 (providing that dividends for capital stocks may not exceed 12%). There are other state statutes that are silent on the issue. *See, e.g.*, ALASKA STAT. § 10.15.095.

an exemption from registration. For example, some states give cooperatives a specific exemption for transactions by cooperative associations (1) that do not involve advertising or public solicitation, and (2) that represent "a contribution of capital to the association by a person who is or intends to become a member or patron of the association," and (3) that is non-transferrable (except in the case of death, operation of law, etc.). [182]

PRACTICAL TIP

Preferred share offerings can be a good way to obtain operating capital. However, they must be carefully considered and implemented to ensure compliance with state and federal securities laws, and to avoid unanticipated tax considerations. Cooperatives should seek legal and tax counsel before issuing preferred shares to members or others.

(d)   Unallocated Equity

The longer that a cooperative does business, the more likely it is that the value of its assets will exceed the stated dollar value of its equity less its debt. This excess is often described as "unallocated equity" because the cooperative has not issued any equity instruments that have a claim on the equity value that it represents. Unallocated equity can be especially large if cooperative brands and trademarks have grown in value. Pursuant to the federal tax laws governing cooperatives, the unallocated equity in a cooperative belongs to its members in accordance with their historic patronage, and it must be distributed

---

[182] WASH. REV. CODE § 21.20.320(16).

to the members on this basis in the event that the cooperative liquidates.

Prior to liquidation, a cooperative's unallocated equity capital can serve several important functions. It serves as a cushion that prevents write-downs in the value of cooperative equity. It can also be used in emergency situations to replace allocated equity capital, or to return allocated equity to the cooperative's members on an accelerated schedule. Unallocated capital can also serve as a source of working capital for the cooperative.

(e)   Distinction between Stock Cooperatives and Non-Stock Cooperatives

The distinction between stock cooperatives and non-stock cooperatives is almost entirely formalistic. Most state laws allow cooperatives to be organized as either stock-based or non-stock-based. In stock cooperatives, patrons receive a share certificate that entitles the holder to voting and profit allocation rights upon joining the cooperative and paying all membership fees, if applicable. Non-stock cooperatives issue membership certificates upon such initial payment and entitle the holder to the same rights as a share certificate.[183]

Similar to stock cooperatives, non-stock cooperatives can also issue different types of membership certificates. These capital certificates share many features with preferred stock, in that, they typically do not confer voting rights on their holders, they may bear interest, and they may or may not have a due date.[184] When they do bear

---

[183] *See* Rapp & Ely, USDA Cooperative Info. Report No. 7, *How to Start a Cooperative* 7 (reprint 2010) (rev. 1996), http://www.rurdev.usda.gov/rbs/pub/cir7/cir7.pdf.

[184] *See id.* at 8.

interest, the rate of return is usually fixed. Many state statutes cap the rate of return at 8% of stated value or less.[185] Regardless of whether issued as stock or membership certificates, these units of ownership are typically non-transferable, and may be limited in voting power to comply with the one-member, one-vote principle.[186]

Within these equity structures, variations exist to the meet unique needs and accomplish specific goals of cooperatives. For instance, cooperatives can issue sub-classes of stock or certificates to grant groups of patrons in different geographical areas the right to elect specified seats on the board of directors. Cooperatives considering a unique equity structure should consult an experienced cooperative attorney to ensure compliance with federal and state tax laws.

---

[185] *See, e.g.,* WASH. REV. CODE § 23.86.160; for a discussion on limits on interest in various states, *see* Lynn Pitman, University Of Wisconsin Center For Cooperatives, Staff Paper No. 7, *Limited Cooperative Association Statutes: An Update* (2008).

[186] The rules regarding transferability are complex. Sometimes, restrictions on transferability are the result of statutes. At other times, they are the product of a cooperative's bylaws and are based on broad principles of a cooperative. For specific rules concerning transferability or non-transferability, please contact a reputable attorney with experience in cooperative law.

PRACTICAL TIP

While cooperatives have different limitations on the "equity" they hold, it is essential that they have some operating capital. Members often press to distribute all net income (profit) to them as patronage. However, the board must consult with financial management and advisors to ensure there is enough operating cash on hand to stay in business. Does the company need a certain level of "equity" to operate? Are sufficient reserves on hand for bad times? Does the cooperative have sufficient operating loans available? What minimum equity requirements have been imposed by the banks (called, "covenants")?

Therefore, while the cooperative can and should distribute patronage dividends, responsible ones must determine how much to retain. This is best done by a proactive base capital plan, in which the board decides how much patronage to distribute in advance. This will help manage member pressure to distribute all patronage in good times, while not saving enough for the inevitable bad times.

Section 5.2   Debt

The second means through which a cooperative obtains capital is through debt. Such debt may be long- or short-term, with short-term denoting a period of one year or less. Such debt may include loans, bonds, governmental programs, and other financial instruments from lenders. The level of debt needed by a cooperative will depend on the cooperative's activities and its line of business. As such, cooperatives of different sizes and concentrations will tend to require different levels of debt for their capital needs. For example, while it may be possible for a small cooperative to rely solely on contributions from its members to operate, a large, capital-intensive cooperative, such as an electric or telephone services cooperative, will likely need to issue significant amounts of debt to finance its operations.[187]

The sources and processes through which a cooperative secures debt are, for the most part, similar to the sources and processes through which an ordinary business accesses debt. Customarily, both must agree to certain conditions, restrictions, and requirements. However, a cooperative may have access to unique sources of funding, depending on the cooperative. For example, agricultural cooperatives may secure loans from the offices of U.S. Department of Agriculture's Rural Development. [188] Other unique sources include CoBank,[189] (which is itself a cooperative), and programs by commercial banks, farm credit banks, credit unions, and insurance companies.

Cooperative may find it difficult to obtain debt financing early in their life cycles. Most lenders rely on historical business performance as a metric for predicting the future growth and viability of an enterprise. Without multiple years of business records, cooperatives may need to rely more heavily on equity financing to begin or expand operations.

After a cooperative has been in business for a period of time, it should be easier to obtain short-term loans.

---

[187] *See* Charles T. Autry & Roland F. Hall, *Law of Cooperatives* 74, 77 (12th ed. 2009).

[188] *See* Rapp, *supra* note 133, at 9.

[189] CoBank is part of the Farm Credit System, which was created in the early 1900s by the U.S. Congress to provide credit to farmers and which is administered by the Farm Credit Administration. *See* Autry, *supra* note 137, at 78.

Short-term loans are usually combined with member equity to meet an existing cooperative's working capital needs.[190] Sources of short-term funding include, but are not limited to, credit unions, commercial banks, banks for cooperatives in the farm credit system, and the National Cooperative Bank.[191]

Financing issues should be addressed prior to formation, or as early as is possible afterward, in order to ensure the ongoing success and viability of the cooperative.

Section 5.3   Redemption of Patrons' Equities

Equity redemption is a unique feature of cooperatives that refers to the process in which a cooperative redeems patrons' equities previously issued to members. The redemption of patrons' equities serves two important functions. On the one hand, redemptions maintain proportionality between equity accounts and the actual use of, and business done with, the cooperative by its members. This ensures that the responsibility to finance the cooperative is fairly apportioned amongst a cooperative's members, commensurate with their use.[192] On the other hand, because patrons' equities are usually non-transferable and illiquid and grant no rights to distributions, cooperatives often feel great pressure from members to return equity through redemptions. Against this backdrop, a cooperative should, in accordance with best practices, institute a program to redeem patrons' equities on a regular basis.

Whether a cooperative is legally required to return allocated equity depends on the applicable state statutes, as

---

[190] *See* Rapp, *supra* note 133, at 9.
[191] *See id.*
[192] *See* CAL. CORP. CODE § 12201.

well as federal tax laws. With respect to states, some state cooperative statutes require retained equity to be returned, while others are silent on the subject.[193] No state statute mandates specific requirements.[194] A cooperative, where statutorily permitted, can also pre-emptively address the issue of redeeming equity in its bylaws. Even when state statutes fail to address redemption, it is generally expected, and advisable, for a cooperative to have a system in place. A cooperative that routinely declines to distribute patrons' equities runs the risk of being subjected to an abuse of discretion lawsuit in a court of law. This is also true for a board of directors of a cooperative who return patrons' equities in an unequitable manner.[195] However, it should be noted that an action taken by the board of directors in connection with redemption that serves a reasonable purpose will probably be sanctioned pursuant to the business judgment rule as discussed in Chapter III.[196]

Redemption programs are usually classified under two categories, namely: (1) special equity redemption programs; and (2) systemic equity redemption programs. The key differences between these two categories are explained below.

---

[193] For the states that do, the method, timing, and other technical details for returning allocated equity is left to the discretion of the board of directors of the cooperative or to be set forth in the cooperative's bylaws. *See* Autry, *supra* note 137, at 83.

[194] *See* Robert C. Rathbone & Roger A. Wissman, USDA Agricultural Cooperative Service, ACS Research Report No. 124, *Equity Redemption and Member Equity Allocation Practices of Agricultural Cooperatives* 1 (1993), http://www.rurdev.usda.gov/supportdocuments/rr124.pdf.

[195] *See* Autry, *supra* note 137, at 83.

[196] Legal actions by members of cooperatives alleging abuse of discretion in connection with equity redemption decisions rarely succeed. *See* Autry, *supra* note 137, at 83.

(a)   Special Equity Redemption Programs

Special equity redemption programs redeem patrons' equities upon the occurrence of specified events affecting members. Common triggering events include death, retirement, hardship, reaching a prescribed age, or leaving the underlying business.[197] The advantage of special equity redemption programs is that they are easy to understand and administer. The cooperative also has the power to specify the triggering event. However, because the triggering event often occurs near the end of a member's life, such programs generally are less popular amongst a cooperative's youngest members.

(b)   Systemic Equity Redemption Programs

The following are the three major types of systemic equity redemption programs: (1) revolving fund plan; (2) base capital plan; and (3) percent-of-all-equities program.

(i)   Revolving Fund Plan

A revolving fund plan is the program most commonly used by cooperatives. It is a plan under which patrons' equities are redeemed after a fixed number of years on a first-in, first-out basis.[198] The decision to redeem patrons' equities under the revolving fund plan is prescribed by the cooperative's bylaws, but usually turns on the discretion of the board of directors. This gives the board of directors the power to alter the redemption plan (such as lengthening the period for redemption) in response to changing financial conditions. However, some cooperatives prohibit significant amendments to their revolving

---

[197] *See* Rathbone, *supra* note 143, at 15-16.
[198] *See id.* at 10.

fund plan regardless of the cooperative's financial situation at the time of redemption.

The revolving fund plan is easy to understand and administer, but also may result in inequities between patrons' equities and proportional use.

(ii)   Base Capital Plan

A base capital plan attempts to remedy the proportionality problem that can affect revolving fund plans by making a member's required investment proportional to the member's use of the goods and services of the cooperative. The cooperative, after determining its capital needs for the upcoming year, allocates such capital needs among members in proportion to each member's use of the cooperative during a prior, specified base period. If a member is "over-invested," because the member's use of the cooperative has decreased during a year, then that member receives a greater percentage of cash in its patronage dividend. In contrast, if a member's business with the cooperative has increased during a year, then the member will be "under-invested" and more of the member's patronage dividend will be paid in the form of patrons' equities. This allows a cooperative to build equity without requesting additional capital from its members.

Because the mechanisms and calculations used in a base capital plan can be complex, cooperatives that wish to explore implementing a base capital plan should consult with an experienced cooperative attorney.

(iii)   Percent-of-all-Equities Program

Few cooperatives employ the percent-of-all-equities program. In this method, a cooperative's board of directors establishes a percent of patrons' equities to be redeemed, irrespective of the year they were issued.

The advantage of such a program is that every member receives a redemption amount regardless of the cooperative's performance. For this reason, newer and younger members tend to find this plan most attractive. This plan is also easy to administer and understand, and works well with cooperatives with established membership and patronage. However, this plan can be problematic if the cooperative needs to build large amounts of capital or if it fails to be profitable.

PRACTICAL TIP

Members increase, decrease and stop doing business with the cooperative from time to time. Since their "equity" is often a function of the amount of business they do, it too will fluctuate.

As members leave the cooperative, their "equity" must be bought back ("redeemed"). This can wreak havoc on the cooperative's finances. Some cooperatives mitigate this risk by redeeming (or "retiring" equity over time.)

A proactive base capital plan gives the board a yardstick to measure cash patronage demands in down years, when capital preservation is both most important and hardest to maintain. A proactive base capital plan helps moderate the effects of equity redemption and should be part of all cooperative board discussions.

CHAPTER VI
MERGERS AND ACQUISITIONS

Section 6.1   Introduction

In today's challenging business climate, cooperatives formed dozens of years ago often find that the scope of their work and geographic range of the business has extended beyond the original intent of the cooperative. Others face competitive pressures that force them to work together with other cooperatives or businesses in order to compete against national or international businesses. Like other businesses, cooperatives can merge, acquire, or combine with other businesses in order to increase competitive strength.

Business combinations are complicated, and involve an intricate overlay of practical, legal and accounting issues that are beyond the scope of this manual. Cooperatives share many of the issues that confront any business in deciding to combine with another business. However, the unique structure and culture of a cooperative creates specific implications for these businesses. Like other businesses as well, cooperatives should consult with accounting and legal counsel early in the process. These cooperative-specific issues are discussed below.

Section 6.2   The Deal Team

As discussed in various other sections, the cooperative form creates unique challenges with regards to confidentiality. The patron-owner and democratic control principles of cooperatives mean that board members often feel compelled to disclose information to other members whom they represent. At the same time, board members have a fiduciary duty to the cooperative itself to act with the same type of diligence, loyalty and care that they would in their own affairs. Like other major events for their own businesses, it is essential to maintain confidentiality with regards to any merger or acquisition. One of the ways to maintain confidentiality is to limit the number of people who are "in the know." Other corporations will often create a specific "deal team" that will be comprised of a very limited number of people who will focus on analyzing the potential transaction. By limiting the number of individuals who have access, the corporation can limit the risk of disclosure, thereby maintaining a competitive advantage.

So who should be part of the deal team? Typically for cooperatives, the transaction team would include the chief executive officer, chief financial officer, chairperson of the board of directors, and one or more outside directors. [199] By maintaining a small deal team and operational control, the cooperative can assess whether a merger is appropriate from a business perspective.

---

[199] Outside directors refer to non-member directors. Many cooperatives permit the engagement of business professionals outside of the cooperative in order to provide expertise that may not be available within the member base.

> ### PRACTICAL TIP
>
> *A merger is one of the most significant business decisions most cooperative board members will ever make. It affects their own business and the businesses and lives of all other members. Never are the duties of confidentiality and avoiding conflicts of interest more important. Board members should also consider engaging outside advisors, such as business acquisition specialists, to assist them throughout the transaction.*

Section 6.3   Alternative Structures

Before determining that two cooperatives should merge, the deal team (describe above) should carefully analyze alternatives to a formal merger. The formal merger is, of course, very difficult to unwind if it ends up not providing the benefits anticipated before the transaction. As such, it is often helpful to consider other forms of cooperation that can occur between the organizations before determining whether a full merger is appropriate.

Cooperation Agreements. Like other businesses, cooperatives can simply agree to work together on certain aspects of their business with other organizations. For example, two cooperatives might agree to share certain resources or marketing expenditures on a collaborative basis.

Joint Ventures. Even absent a merger, cooperatives can and often do engage in joint activities with each other. Joint ventures can be a good method to determine whether cooperation on other matters can exist. Joint ventures typically fall into two categories. First, two cooperatives can enter into a written contract for a joint venture that would be jointly managed by both organizations. Second, the cooperatives could create a subsidiary that is partially owned by each cooperative.[200] The corporate joint venture would create a separate entity subject to all legal formalities.

Hybrid or Federated Cooperative. As discussed in Section 1.4 above, a cooperative can be comprised of multiple cooperatives, known as either federated or hybrid cooperatives. Consequently, instead of a formal merger, cooperatives can consider the creation of a super structure cooperative, which would be owned by the two cooperatives who otherwise considered merging. It may, however, have tax implications depending on how the hybrid is designed.

Cross Licensing Agreements. Before merging, cooperatives can consider cross-licensing their technology, brand or other intellectual property.

Cross Marketing Agreements. Marketing cooperatives can consider joint marketing or cooperative-based advertising as part of an overall integration strategy.

Wind-Up. Instead of a formal merger, the target cooperative could also simply wind-up its operations and allow its membership to become members of the acquiring entity. This would, however, create significant potential exposure to the last few members of the dissolving cooperative, who would be responsible for any liabilities of the closing cooperative.

---

[200] In addition, the joint venture could get financing through non-cooperative entities or individuals as well.

As discussed above, the options should be considered in the context of the particular practical, legal and accounting ramifications of each business type before moving forward.

Section 6.4 Special Laws Regulating Cooperative Mergers

State cooperative laws can set forth specific rules to govern the merger process. Many state statutes place limitations on the type of business organizations that cooperatives are allowed to merge with. Some states only permit a cooperative to merge with another cooperative. [201] Other states, such as Washington, only authorize cooperatives to merge with other domestic cooperatives or domestic ordinary business corporations.[202] Some states, on the other hand, permit their cooperatives to merge with any cooperatives or for-profit business entities, foreign or domestic.[203]

To begin the merger process, the board of directors must approve a plan of merger. State cooperatives statutes identify the specific information that the plan of merger must contain. In Washington, for example, the plan of merger must include the following information:[204]

- The names of the associations proposing to merge.

---

[201] *See, e.g.,* MINN. STAT. ANN. § 308A.801 (permitting merger with a cooperative or another entity operating on a cooperative plan, either foreign or domestic); WIS. STAT. § 185.61(1)(a) (permitting a cooperative to merge with a cooperative formed in Wisconsin or in any other state).

[202] WASH. REV. CODE § 23.86.220(1).

[203] CAL. CORP. CODE § 12530; OR. REV. STAT. § 62.617(1).

[204] WASH. REV. CODE § 23.86.220(2). For other states' requirements for the plan of merger, *see* CAL. CORP. CODE § 12531; MINN. STAT. ANN. § 308A.801 subdiv. 2; OR. REV. STAT. § 62.617(2); WIS. STAT. § 185.61(1)(b).

- The name of the association which is to be the surviving association in the merger.

- The terms and conditions of the merger.

- The manner and basis of converting the shares of each merging association into shares or other securities or obligations of the surviving association.

- A statement of any changes in the articles of incorporation of the surviving association to be effected by such merger.

- Such other provisions with respect to the proposed merger as are deemed necessary or desirable.

The board must mail a written notice to each member of the cooperative that contains the full text of the plan of merger and the time and place of the meeting at which the members will vote on the plan of merger.[205] The plan of merger must be approved by a vote of the cooperative's members. Many state cooperatives statutes require the affirmative vote of two-thirds of the votes cast (or a greater proportion if provided in the articles or bylaws) to approve the plan of merger.[206] Several other state cooperatives statutes require a simple majority of the votes cast (or a greater proportion if provided in the articles or bylaws) to approve the plan of merger.[207]

---

[205] *See* MINN. STAT. ANN. § 308A.801 subdiv. 3; OR. REV. STAT. § 62.619(1)(a); WASH. REV. CODE § 23.86.220(3); WIS. STAT. § 185.61(2)(a). The California cooperatives statute does not include an explicit notice requirement. *See* CAL. CORP. CODE § 12533(a).

[206] *See, e.g.*, MINN. STAT. ANN. § 308A.801 subdiv. 4(2); WASH. REV. CODE § 23.86.220(3); WIS. STAT. § 185.61(2)(b).

[207] *See, e.g.*, CAL. CORP. CODE § 12224, 12533(a); OR. REV. STAT. § 62.619(1)(a).

Once the members of the cooperative have adopted the plan of merger, the cooperative must file articles of merger with the Secretary of State. State statutes differ on the information that must be disclosed in the articles of merger. In Washington, for example, the articles of merger must contain the following information:[208]

- The plan of merger.

- As to each association, the number of members and, if there is capital stock, the number of shares outstanding.

- As to each association, the number of members who voted for and against such plan.

The merger can be abandoned at any time before the articles of merger are filed with the Secretary of State.[209] The merger takes place on the effective date of the merger (generally when the articles of merger are filed with the Secretary of State), at which time the parties to the plan of merger become a single entity and the separate existence of all parties other than the surviving entity will cease.[210] The surviving entity possesses all the rights and property of the merged entities and, depending on applicable law, may be subject to all their obligations and liabilities.[211]

---

[208] WASH. REV. CODE § 23.86.220(4). For the contents of the articles of merger in other states, *see* CAL. CORP. CODE § 12535; MINN. STAT. ANN. § 308A.801 subdiv. 4(b); OR. REV. STAT. § 62.621(1); WIS. STAT. § 185.62(1).

[209] *See* CAL. CORP. CODE § 12537; MINN. STAT. ANN. § 308A.801 subdiv. 4(e); OR. REV. STAT. § 62.619(2); WASH. REV. CODE § 23.86.220(9); WIS. STAT. § 185.61(5).

[210] *See* CAL. CORP. CODE § 12535; MINN. STAT. ANN. § 308A.801 subdiv. 5(a); OR. REV. STAT. § 62.623; WASH. REV. CODE § 23.86.230; WIS. STAT. § 185.62(2).

[211] *See* CAL. CORP. CODE § 12550; MINN. STAT. ANN. § 308A.

Section 6.5 Post-Merger Taxation, Ownership and Patronage

Cooperative members often have a simplistic view of the equity and tax implications of a merger, especially when they are in a small industry or geographically close to the other entity. Why can't they just combine forces, swap out each others' equity, and call it good?

In addition to cash on hand, retained earnings, or the "equity" on the books of a cooperative, all entities have value in the ongoing nature of their operations, the value of their customer and member lists, and the goodwill that the entity has built. These create taxable value that is transferred by the cooperatives to each other, resulting in a "net" value that one obtains over the other. Put simply, the IRS believes that it is rarely, if ever, possible to have a true "merger of equals." Instead, the IRS requires each entity to identify the value of their cooperative as of the merger date. They look at either the "acquisition method" (determining who acquired whom) or the "book method" (determining the book value of each entity).

The tax treatment and implications of a merger are unique to the situation and beyond the scope of this manual. Each party to a potential merger should engage experienced cooperative tax counsel well before the merger is to be effective in order to understand the implications of various forms and timing of merger.

> ## PRACTICAL TIP
>
> *While phrased "post-merger tax issues," those issues must be considered long before the merger is contemplated. Tax issues often drive the form of combination and, in some cases, whether it makes sense to do at all.*

CHAPTER VII
PRICING AND COMPETITION

Section 7.1 Antitrust Law in General

Antitrust law is based on the premise that competitive markets (or at least markets free from artificial restraints on competition) will better promote the interests of consumers.[212] At least one commentator described the purpose of antitrust laws as the maintenance of a workably competitive marketplace by eliminating anti-competitive market conduct and market structures.[213] When implemented correctly, both antitrust laws and market regulation serve to facilitate market efficiency.[214] An understanding of – and compliance with – antitrust law is imperative for the board members and executives of any business.

Antitrust law is divided primarily into two parts. One part prohibits agreements that unreasonably restrain trade. Some agreements are illegal *per se* (that is, automatically, without any consideration of actual market effects) from

---

[212] *Leegin Creative Leather Prods., Inc. v. PSKS, Inc.*, 551 U.S. 877 (2007) ("In its design and function the rule [of reason] distinguishes between restraints with anticompetitive effect that are harmful to the consumer and restraints stimulating competition that are in the consumer's best interest.").

[213] Stacey L. Dogan & Mark A. Lemley, *Antitrust Law and Regulatory Gaming*, 87 Tex. L. Rev. 685, 695 n. 51 (2009) (citing Stephen Breyer, Regulation and Its Reform, 156-57 (1982)).

[214] *Id.*

the specific agreement).[215] Agreements that fall into this category include agreements between competition that fix the price at which they will sell their products ("price-fixing"), that restrict output, or that allocate customers or territories. Other agreements (such as agreements between a supplier and its reseller) are reviewed on a facts-and-circumstances basis to determine whether, on balance, they are anticompetitive. A second branch of antitrust law prohibits monopolization and attempted monopolization. For example, if a firm with very large market share in an industry that is hard to enter tries to exclude rivals, that large firm faces antitrust risk.[216]

As discussed in Chapter II, cooperatives are often formed to jointly market or purchase, in an effort to get better prices. So the question becomes, might a cooperative itself be anticompetitive?

> ### *PRACTICAL TIP*
> *Remember that antitrust concerns can arise any time an entity has a dominant market in a specific geography. Antitrust is not limited to price domination in national marketplace.*

Section 7.2   Capper-Volstead Act

The Capper-Volstead Act of 1922 ("CVA") permits a qualified cooperative and its members to jointly process, prepare, and advertise their products in the marketplace, notwithstanding the antitrust laws.[217] The Act was passed,

---

[215] *Leegin*, 551 U.S. at 886 ("The *per se* rule, treating categories of restraints as necessarily illegal, eliminates the need to study the reasonableness of an individual restraint in light of the real market forces at work. . . .").

[216] Other parts of antitrust law (such as the law relating to mergers and acquisitions and the law relating to price discrimination) are not covered in this booklet.

[217] 7 U.S.C. §§ 291-292.

in part, from fear that the Sherman Act could be en-
forced to prevent farmers from engaging in the cooperative activity that was critical to their economic survival.[218]
Although businessmen could pool money to form corporations rich with resources and leverage, farmers' efforts to establish cooperatives were thwarted by the
looming threat of litigation under federal antitrust law.
Before the CVA's passage, Congress had attempted to
remedy the situation by enacting Section 6 of the Clayton
Act of 1914,[219] providing an exemption for agricultural
and horticultural organizations.[220] This exemption ulti-
mately proved inadequate, failing to specify the types of
activities that a cooperative could permissibly engage in
and still be shielded from antitrust liability.[221] Eventually,
the much needed guidance was provided when the CVA
was enacted to level the playing field between farmers
and large businesses by extending broader protection
from the antitrust law.[222] Fisheries are covered by the federal Fishery Marketing Cooperative Act of 1934.[223]

The past few years have seen a rash of litigation over the
scope of the CVA, involving agricultural cooperatives in
a range of agricultural products.[224] These cases raise both

---

[218] *Loewe v. Lawlor*, 208 U.S. 274, 301 (1908) (noting that "[t]he act made no distinction between classes. It provided that 'every' contract, combination or conspiracy
in restraint of trade was illegal. The records of Congress show that several efforts
were made to exempt, by legislation, organizations of farmers and laborers from
the operation of the act and that all these efforts failed, so that act remained as we
have it before us.")
[219] 15 U.S.C. § 17.
[220] *Id.*
[221] *Id.*
[222] *See* 61 Cong. Rec. 1033 (1921) (statement of Rep. Volstead); 62 Cong. Rec. 2057
(1922) (statement of Rep. Capper).
[223] 15 U.S.C. §§ 521-522.
[224] *See, e.g., In re Processed Egg Prods. Antitrust Litig.*, 931 F. Supp. 2d 654 (E.D. Pa. 2013);
In re Se. Milk Antitrust Litig., No. 2:07-CV-208, 2013 U.S. Dist. LEXIS 18928 (E.D.
Tenn. Jan. 22, 2013), *settled in* 2013 U.S. Dist. LEXIS 70163 (E.D. Tenn., May 17,
2013); *Allen v. Dairy Farmers of Am., Inc.*, No. 5:09-cv-230, 2013 WL 211303 (D.

substantive and procedural implications for cooperatives, and they reinforce the importance of cooperatives' staying abreast of recent developments to ensure compliance with the CVA's stringent requirements. In particular, cooperative managers and directors must understand which business practices and kinds of conduct may expose their organization to antitrust liability and what steps they must take to qualify for CVA protection. Because of the recent advances in an otherwise complex area of the law, this guide attempts to organize and condense the CVA and the cases in a way that is useful.

To be protected under the CVA, a defendant/cooperative must comply with a variety of requirements, all of which can be addressed by asking two broad-based questions. First, is the cooperative the type of organization covered by the CVA? Second, are the organization's activities at issue protected by the CVA antitrust exemption? All CVA-related questions should be examined within this analytical framework to adequately assess the risk of potential antitrust liability.

(a) Structural Requirements

To qualify for antitrust protection, the CVA requires that (1) every member of the cooperative be a "producer" of agricultural products; and (2) the cooperative have the prescribed structure and operate in the prescribed manner.

Vt. Jan. 18, 2013); *Edwards, et al. v. National Milk Producers Fed'n, et al.*, No. 11-04766 (N.D. Cal. filed Sept. 26, 2011); *In re Mushroom Direct Purchaser Antitrust Litig.*, No. 06-0620, 2012 U.S. Dist. LEXIS 151171 (E.D. Pa. Oct. 22, 2012); *In re Fresh & Process Potatoes Antitrust Litig.*, No. 4:10-MD-2186-BLW, 2012 U.S. Dist. LEXIS 139440 (D. Idaho Aug. 31, 2012); *Stephen L. LaFrance Holding Inc. v. National Milk Producers Fed'n*, No. 12-70, 2012 WL 3104416 (E.D. Pa. July 31, 2012).

> **PRACTICAL TIP**
>
> *Price control maintenance is essential for many agricultural cooperatives. They may need to attain a dominant market position in order to effectively compete. Cooperative board members should become familiar with the opportunities and limitations of the Capper-Volstead Act ("CVA") and make sure they analyze competition issues with each new business line or transaction.*

(i)   All Members Must be Agricultural Producers

To qualify for CVA protection, *all* members of the cooperative must be "producers" of "agricultural products."[225] The CVA itself provides a non-exhaustive list of qualifying producers: farmers, planters, ranchmen, dairymen, and nut or fruit growers.[226] The general principle is that pure "processors" (that is, persons or companies that do not produce farm products) cannot be members if the cooperative wants CVA protection. The Supreme Court has reinforced the broad application of this rule by holding that even if a cooperative includes "non-producer" members, the cooperative will not have CVA protection.[227] Some lower courts have applied a somewhat less stringent rule, permitting a cooperative to keep its CVA status where a small number of non-producers are admitted (or kept on the membership rolls) through

---

[225] 7 U.S.C. § 291.

[226] *Id.*

[227] *National Broiler Mktg. Ass'n v. U.S.* ("*NBMA*"), 436 U.S. 816, 828 (1978) (out of as many as 75 members, "six NBMA members do not own or control any breeder flock whose offspring are raised as broilers, and do not own or control any hatchery where the broiler chicks are hatched . . . [a]nd . . . three members do not own a breeder flock or hatchery, and also do not maintain any grow-out facility"). *See also Case-Swayne Co. v. Sunkist Growers, Inc.*, 389 U.S. 384 (1967).

administrative oversight, so long as they do not participate in the decision making aspects of the cooperative.[228]
Likewise, CVA protection will not be lost if otherwise
ineligible processors obtain a limited role in the cooperative (for example, by lending money or by acquiring
non-voting preferred shares).[229] A more recent case, however, has held that the membership of even one non-producer legal entity destroyed the cooperative's CVA status.[230]

(1) Vertically Integrated Busi-
nesses

A business is "integrated" if it is involved in more than
one stage of production.[231] Many *bona fide* producers are
"integrated" because they engage in downstream activities such as sorting, packing, processing, or marketing.
Some courts have found treating "integrated" firms as
producers is crucial because the nature of agriculture has
changed significantly since the CVA's enactment, and
vertical integration has become a necessary part of what
a "producer" must do.[232] Other courts, however, do not
agree that all integrated producers qualify as "producers." These courts suggest instead a case-by-case analysis
to determine the extent to which "the nature of the association's activities, the degree of integration of its
members, and the functions historically performed by

---

[228] *Alexander v. National Farmers Org.*, 687 F.2d 1173, 1185-87 (8th Cir. 1982).

[229] *Case-Swayne Co. v. Sunkist Growers, Inc.*, 355 F. Supp. 408, 415 (C.D. Cal. 1971).

[230] *In re Mushroom Direct Purchaser Antitrust Litig.*, 621 F. Supp. 2d 274, 284 (E.D. Pa. 2009), *appeal dismissed*, 655 F.3d 158 (3d Cir. 2011) (noting lower court's holding that "EMMC was not a proper agricultural cooperative under the Capper-Vol-stead Act because one member . . . was not technically a grower of agricultural produce.").

[231] *See United States v. Hinote*, 823 F. Supp. 1350, 1353 (S.D. Miss. 1993).

[232] *NBMA*, 436 U.S. at 840 (White, J., dissenting). The majority in *NBMA* expressly chose not to address the issue of whether fully integrated agribusiness would be disqualified under the CVA. *Id.* at 828 n. 21.

farmers in the industry are relevant considerations in deciding whether an association is exempt."[233]

Most recently, courts have built on this second, fact-intensive approach using a two-step analysis.[234] The first step is a fact-based inquiry that focuses on the economics and history of the relevant industry, the functions of each association, and the degree of integration of each participant.[235] The second step is a determination of whether membership is consistent with the legislative intent of creating an environment in which farmers can compete on a level playing field.[236]

Regardless of which approach is followed, a business that is purely a processor never falls within CVA protection.[237] Accordingly, all non-producers that solely engage in (for example) packaging or marketing are not qualified to be members of a CVA-protected cooperative.

(ii)   Foreign Producers

The CVA does not restrict cooperative membership to U.S. producers, and two courts have found that a domestic cooperative can include foreign producers as members or can cooperate with foreign producer organizations without losing CVA status.[238] If the foreign producer organization does not satisfy CVA requirements, however, the relationship with that producer organization is not protected under CVA.

---

[233] *Id.* at 836 (Brennan, J., concurring).
[234] *In re Fresh & Process Potatoes*, 834 F. Supp. 2d at 1154.
[235] *Id.* at 1154
[236] *Id.*
[237] *NBMA*, 436 U.S. at 822; *In re Fresh & Process Potatoes*, 834 F. Supp. 2d 1141, 1152 (D. Idaho 2011).
[238] *In re Fresh & Process Potatoes*, 834 F. Supp. 2d at 1158.

(b)   Organizational Structure

A second structural requirement mandates that (1) the association is operated for the mutual benefit of its members as producers, and (2) that at least half of its the agricultural products that it handles come from cooperative members. In addition, the cooperative must either operate on a "one-member, one-vote" basis, *or* it must limit capital dividends to 8% or less. These provisions are designed to ensure that qualifying organizations are controlled by and for producers, and are not merely tools of non-producers.

(i)   The Cooperative Must be Operated for the Mutual Benefit of its Members

The requirement that cooperatives are operated for the mutual benefit of its members as producers was designed to insure that all qualifying cooperatives are truly organized and controlled by and for the member producers.[239] This provision serves as assurance that organizations serving a purpose other than the mutual obtaining of a fair return for their producer-members do not have access to the CVA's benefits.[240] Although not specifically defined, the mutual-benefit requirement embodies the idea of farmer control, mandating that – at a minimum – the association serves its producers over any other economic interest.[241]

The "mutual benefit" provision does not limit the types of activities that a cooperative may engage in, or prevent a cooperative from working with third parties (although

---

[239] *Case-Swayne*, 389 U.S. at 394.

[240] *Id.*

[241] L. Gene Lemon, Antitrust and Agricultural Cooperatives Collective Bargaining in the Sale of Agricultural Products, 44 N.D. L. Rev. 505, 510 (1968).

that third-party relationship is not itself protected under the CVA). The CVA only requires the association be operated for the mutual benefit of the members, and courts are wary to impose restrictions beyond those found in the text of the statute.[242] From a practical standpoint, however, by using a third party or agent to carry out production or processing, a cooperative should confirm that it is really engaging in the mutual benefit of its members rather than for the benefit of the third party.

(ii)   Member-Handle Rule – At Least Half of the Products

The CVA's requirement that at least half of the products that a cooperative markets be members' products is also a means to ensure that the cooperative serves the producers ahead of any other economic interest. This rule is indicated in the CVA's legislative history. The rule prevents a small number of wealthy farmers from conspiring to restrain trade in a commodity by forming a cooperative and subsequently purchasing a large share of crop to adversely impact the market.[243] Cooperatives must comply with the member-handle rule[244] on an annual basis. Product purchased from others by the members and then resold through the cooperative is counted as non-member product for calculation purposes.[245]

As long as it complies with the member-handle limitation, a cooperative may deal in the products of non-members on a regular basis. To ensure compliance, a cooperative should adopt record keeping and internal controls that permit the cooperative to know the ratio of

---

[242] *See Agritronics Corp. v. National Dairy Herd Ass'n*, 914 F. Supp. 814 (N.D.N.Y. 1996).
[243] S. Rep. No. 236, at 3 (1921).
[244] 7 U.S.C. § 291.
[245] *See* discussion of "patronage" and "non-patronage" income above.

member to non-member product at any given time – and to be able to demonstrate that it satisfies the requirement.

(iii) One Vote Per Member or Dividends of Less Than 8%

If a cooperative chooses the one-member/one-vote path, the limitation must apply regardless of the amount of stock or membership capital that the member owns. If the cooperative departs from this requirement, then the cooperative cannot pay a capital dividend in excess of 8% each year. Under this model, members may have a variable number of votes, and weighted voting based on patronage is permissible.[246] (Due to other restrictions imposed by various federal and state laws, most cooperatives tend to limit voting to one-vote per one-member *and* restrict capital dividends to below 8%.)

Both the one-member/one-vote rule and the 8% annual dividend cap serve the principle that a cooperative is not an investment vehicle for profit, but rather a venture to achieve common business goals. The dividend cap also seeks to provide members with as much return as possible from the sale of their products.[247] Regardless of which option the cooperative chooses, it is essential that these provisions be built into the foundational documents including the articles of incorporation or the cooperative bylaws to ensure proper documentation of compliance.

---

[246] *Agritronics*, 914 F. Supp. 814.

[247] H.R. 12931, 66th Cong., (2d Sess. 1920); 59 Cong. Rec. 6553 (1920) (statement of Rep. Volstead); 61 Cong. Rec. 1033 (1921) (statement of Rep. Volstead). *See also* Wash. Rev. Code § 23.86.160.

(c)   Membership-Control and Policy-Making

A cooperative loses CVA protection if it includes non-producers as "members," but the CVA does not define membership.[248] Cases have made it reasonably clear that membership accrues when a non-producer participates in the control and policy making of the cooperative.[249]

To determine whether an entity is a member of a cooperative, a court will look past the title or label given to the "member" – in the bylaws, for example – and will consider whether the entity possesses the substantive rights of a member, or has input into the affairs of the association that would be expected of a member.[250] Entities that possess voting power (or equivalent) can control the policy making of the cooperative, and they are therefore likely to be considered "members."[251] In contrast, nominal "members" with no de facto control over a cooperative or influence over the cooperative's policies are not true members, and a court is therefore unlikely to strip a cooperative of its CVA status on this basis.[252] To avoid confusion or controversy, cooperatives should not use the term "member" to describe associated persons that do not have voting rights. Their more limited role should also be described in the cooperative's articles of incorporation or bylaws. Depending on the circumstances, other steps may also be taken to make clear that non-producers do not have the rights of membership.

---

[248] *Case-Swayne*, 389 U.S. at 395-96.

[249] *Id.* at 395.

[250] *Agritronics*, 914 F. Supp. at 824.

[251] *Id.*

[252] *Id.*

(d) Agents, Employees, and Working With Other Cooperatives

Some cooperatives have no employees and operate solely through their members. More commonly, however, a cooperative will have employees and non-employee agents.

A cooperative and its members are free to engage with agents without losing CVA protection. The CVA explicitly allows for the use of agents by stating that "associations may have marketing agencies in common; and such associations and their members may make the necessary contracts and agreements to effect such purposes."[253] Of course, these agreements are subject to the "mutual benefit" limitation described in the statute.

Marketing agents may carry out the same purpose that the cooperative's members perform on behalf of the member producers – or any other functions – including processing, preparing for market, handling, marketing and pricing the members' products.[254] Further, several cooperatives may act together through common marketing agencies to voluntarily eliminate competition amongst themselves without fear of potential antitrust liability.

A cooperative may authorize an agent to act on its behalf subject to the principles of agency law.[255] This power can be created where the cooperative expressly authorizes the agent to act, or causes the agent to believe that he or she has the power to act, or a third party reasonably believes it.[256] Regardless of the activity an agent is engaged to perform, the cooperative should clearly document and explicitly lay out the role and responsibility of the agent

---

[253] 7 U.S.C. § 291.

[254] *Kinnett Dairies, Inc. v. Dairymen, Inc.*, 512 F. Supp. 608, 633 (1981).

[255] *In re Fresh & Process Potatoes*, 834 F. Supp. 2d at 1167.

[256] *Id.*

in acting on the cooperative's behalf, paying close attention to ensure that the cooperative is still engaged for the mutual benefit of its members despite the use of any agent.

Employees of a cooperative member do not have to be producers in an individual capacity – the cooperative itself acts as a single legal entity including its own organization and its employees, agents, and officers. [257] Moreover, employees and other directors and officers may be held liable for antitrust violations for engaging in prohibited conduct in the course of their regular duties.[258]

(i)   Relationships With Other Cooperatives

Producers often pool their resources with other cooperatives to enter lines of business beyond the ability of a single cooperative. CVA protects a "federated" cooperative if its members either are producers or are qualified cooperatives (that is, whose own members are producers).[259] Similarly, several cooperatives may band together to market, bargain, and negotiate contracts for the sale of its product without formally joining together as one cooperative.[260]

(e)   Conduct

The CVA protects farmers from antitrust liability for establishing cooperatives and pursuing normal business

---

[257] *Green v. Associated Milk Producers, Inc.*, 692 F.2d 1153, 1157 (8th Cir. 1982).

[258] *Tillamook Cheese & Dairy Ass'n v. Tillamook Cnty. Creamery Ass'n*, 358 F.2d 115, 118 (9th Cir. 1966). *See also Bergjans Farm Dairy Co. v. Sanitary Milk Producers*, 241 F. Supp. 476, 486 (E.D. Mo. 1965).

[259] *Agritronics*, 914 F. Supp. at 823; *United States v. Maryland Coop. Milk Producers*, 145 F. Supp. 151, 154 (D.D.C. 1956).

[260] *Treasure Valley Potato Bargaining Assoc. v. Ore-Ida Foods, Inc.*, 497 F.2d 203, 215 (9th Cir. 1974).

objectives. It provides farmers, acting through cooperatives, the same advantage and responsibility available to businessmen acting through corporations. [261] Courts recognize that the CVA is intended to enable farmer-producers to organize together, set association policy, fix prices, and otherwise carry on like a corporation without thereby violating federal antitrust laws.[262] In contrast, the CVA does not give cooperatives unrestricted power to restrain trade or engage in monopolization.[263]

(i)   Prohibited Conduct

CVA protection is not unfettered. Qualified cooperatives are prohibited from engaging in three specific types of conduct: (1) conspiring with or combining with non-producer entities in restraint of trade in violation of Section 1 of the Sherman Act; (2) engaging in predatory conduct in violation of Section 2 of the Sherman Act; and (3) unduly enhancing prices.

(1)   Conspiring or Combining With Non-Producers

A cooperative violates Section 1 of the Sherman Act when it conspires with non-cooperative customers to fix the customers' resale price. A court will infer a conspiracy from the cooperative's actions, course of dealing or other circumstances.[264] There is no threshold amount of commerce that must be restrained by a price fixing agreement; a court will strictly enforce liability for any amount price fixing as automatically illegal.[265]

---

[261] *Maryland and Virginia Milk Producers Ass'n v. U.S.*, 362 U.S. 458, 466 (1960).

[262] *Id.* at 466-67.

[263] *Id.*

[264] *Bergjans*, 241 F. Supp. at 482.

[265] *Id.*

(2)   Predatory Conduct

Courts are always skeptical of conduct that can legitimately be described as "predatory" – that is, that does not appear to have a *bona fide* business purpose and is primarily intended to restrain trade or prevent competition.[266] Determining the existence of predatory conduct requires a fact-specific, case-by-case inquiry. Courts have found, in a number of cases, overly aggressive methods of competition to be predatory. For example, the use of intimidation to force unwilling producers to join or abide by the prices and practices of an association may be considered predatory.[267] Pressuring non-affiliated persons to refrain from doing business with certain buyers to force otherwise unwilling buyers to deal with, or abide by prices set by the cooperative is predatory conduct that is not protected under CVA.[268] Covert manipulation of prices paid by buyers through – for example – paying secret rebates to undermine competitors has also been challenged.[269] Similarly, picketing or otherwise disrupting retailers who bought from competing processors, thereby coercing the retailers to buy from those who did secure product from the cooperative, is considered not protected.[270] On the other hand, cooperatives and their members may contract or agree as necessary to carry out organizational purposes.[271] Cooperatives may enforce these agreements so long as the agreements are valid to

[266] *See, e.g., Maryland*, 362 U.S. at 468.
[267] *Alexander*, 687 F.2d at 1182; *Fairdale Farms v. Yankee Milk*, 635 F.2d 1037, 1044 (2d Cir. 1980).
[268] *Maryland*, 362 U.S.at 468.
[269] *Bergjans*, 241 F. Supp. at 484.
[270] *Otto Milk Co. v. United Dairy Farmers Coop. Ass'n*, 261 F. Supp. 381, 385 (W.D. Pa. 1966).
[271] 7 U.S.C. § 291.

begin with and the enforcement does not amount to predatory conduct.[272]

(ii)   Undue Price Enhancement

Section 2 of the CVA establishes an "undue price enhancement" test. If the Secretary of Agriculture finds that a cooperative is monopolizing or restraining trade such that agricultural product prices are unduly enhanced, the Secretary must serve a complaint and notice of hearing for the cooperative.[273] The Secretary has jurisdiction to enforce Section 2 by issuing a cease and desist order and instituting corresponding proceedings. No case law has set an objective standard for when a price is considered "unduly enhanced," and the Secretary has never found a violation. But the courts have made clear that prices set above "competitive" levels are not necessarily "undue."[274]

One recent case has found that the Secretary of Agriculture's powers under CVA Section 2 does not preclude antitrust actions against a cooperative. In the court found that the Secretary of Agriculture does not have exclusive or primary jurisdiction to determine whether conduct is exempted under the Capper-Volstead Act.[275]

---

[272] *See, e.g., Holly Sugar Corp. v. Goshen Cnty. Coop. Beet Growers Ass'n,* 725 F.2d 564 (10th Cir. 1984).

[273] 7 U.S.C. § 292.

[274] *Sunkist Growers v. F.T.C.,* 464 F. Supp. 302, 311 (C.D. Cal. 1979).

[275] *Edwards, et al. v. National Milk Producers Fed'n, et al.,* No. 11-04766 (N.D. Cal. filed Sept. 26, 2011).

(iii) Conduct Permitted but Not Required

Qualifying cooperatives may engage in the processing, preparing for market, handling or marketing of agricultural products. [276] This includes acting as a single association, bargaining, negotiating, and setting prices.

(iv) Pricing

It is well established that price-fixing and output-restrictions are *per-se* illegal.[277] A cooperative that does nothing but set member prices or member output levels faces a severe antitrust risk unless its conduct is protected under the CVA. Cooperatives, however, may engage in joint pricing joint marketing agreements, withholding product from the market, and exchanging price information among a cooperative's members. Cooperatives that undertake significant activity for their members such as processing raw products or marketing products for its members are typically on safer ground than cooperatives that play a more minimal role (such as simply setting a price at which members then sell directly).

(v) Supply Management and Responses to Consumer Demand

Recent litigation has called into question a cooperative's ability to engage in supply management.[278] The court in *In re Fresh and Process Potatoes Antitrust Litigation* held that the CVA does not apply to pre-production output restrictions. [279] Rather, it only applies after products are

---

[276] 7 U.S.C. § 291.
[277] *See, e.g., United States v. Joint Traffic Ass'n*, 171 U.S. 505 (1898); *Standard Oil Co. v. U.S.*, 221 U.S. 1 (1911).
[278] *In re Fresh & Process Potatoes*, 834 F. Supp. 2d at 1154.
[279] *Id.* at 1157.

planted (and possibly only after the products are harvested).[280]

Some commentators suggest that the court's holding in this case is inconsistent with the express language of the statute, as well as the congressional intent and legislative history behind the CVA.[281] Others argue that an individual farmer's uninhibited ability to control its own production serves as a natural check on cooperatives, because as prices rise, farmers will produce more output – which imposes a practical limit on the cooperative's ability to increase prices without provoking excess production.[282]

Section 7.3 Limited Cooperative Act Entities (LCAs)

Agricultural producers may organize as Limited Cooperative Act entities. However, the primary benefit of LCAs is to allow for investor-members. LCAs that permit investor members would most likely not meet the structural requirements of the Capper-Volstead Act, so would lose the protection that statute affords.[283] Agricultural producers should consult with legal counsel before adopting an LCA structure for their cooperative.

---

[280] *Id.* at 1155.
[281] *Id.*
[282] *Id.* at 1156.
[283] *Compare*, Section 7.2(a).

CHAPTER VIII
EMPLOYMENT LAW

As a corporation organized under state law, cooperatives are generally subject to all employment laws and regulations. The myriad requirements of these statutes are beyond the scope of this book; however, there are two issues peculiar to cooperatives.

Section 8.1   Size of Cooperative Will Determine Which Statutes Apply

Whether a particular employment law applies will depend on the number of employees engaged by that individual employer. A cooperative's governing law will depend on the number of employees that cooperative engages, not counting any employees solely engaged by its members. In other words, only the employees of the cooperative are considered when determining coverage. For example, employers of all sizes are covered by state workers' compensation and unemployment insurance laws. Therefore, all cooperatives will be governed by them. However, only employers of eight or more employees are covered by the Washington Law Against Discrimination. Therefore, a small cooperative (for example, with only five employees) will not be covered by the WLAD, even if its members collectively employ hundreds of workers.

> ## PRACTICAL TIP
>
> *Cooperatives have employees like other businesses, and in most respects these employees are treated the same as with any other corporate form. However, there are key differences for cooperatives. First, employees interact with members as customers, and often can develop deep relationships with the members. Management must interact with employees recognizing these relationships, but also ensuring efficient operations. This is a delicate balance.*

Section 8.2   Multistate Employers and Employees

Cooperative members are often in states other than where the cooperative is located. For example, if an apple marketing cooperative is located in Oregon, but it has sales representatives in Washington, which law applies to those workers?

Generally speaking, the law of the state in which the worker was working at the time will apply to any claims brought by the employee. For example, in 2007 the Washington Supreme Court ruled that "hours worked" for overtime purposes may include hours worked outside the state of Washington. In *Bostain v. Food Express, Inc.,* an employer claimed that it was not required to pay one of its employees overtime because, while the employee averaged 48 hours of work each week, his work inside the state of Washington never exceeded 40 hours per week. [284] The court disagreed, holding that under the WMWA, the driver was entitled to overtime based on all

---

[284] *Bostain v. Food Express, Inc.,* 159 Wn.2d 700 (2007). The driver spent sixty-three percent of his hours working outside the state of Washington.

hours worked, whether within Washington State or out-side the state.[285] Likewise, the California Labor Code ap-plies to overtime work performed in California by out-of-state residents.[286] In *Sullivan*, the California Supreme Court held that the daily overtime requirement for non-exempt employees applies to Colorado-resident workers who were temporarily working in California, even though they would not be entitled to daily overtime in their home state. Consequently, cooperative employers must remain aware of the jurisdictions in which their em-ployees are performing work, and comply with applica-ble laws of those jurisdictions as well as the state in which the cooperative is based.

Section 8.3   No Stock or Options for Employees

Most corporations can freely offer capital stock or op-tions as a part of their compensation packages. Often stock (either directly, or as options) is a major part of the compensation packages of senior executives, because it aligns executive compensation with increases in share value.

Cooperatives, however, can only offer equity to mem-bers who also use their services. In other words, they cannot include stock or options as part of their incentive packages. Cooperatives have less compensation alternatives than other companies, which can make them less competitive when recruiting key talent (*e.g.*, Vice President and above). Cooperatives often look to other compensation vehicles such as phantom stock (cash-

---

[285] *Id.* (by definition, an interstate trucker will spend some hours driving outside Washington State and the WMWA makes no distinction between the hours spent driving in state and those spent driving outside Washington).

[286] *Sullivan v. Oracle Corp.*, 51 Cal. 4th 1191, 1206 (2011).

based bonus that tracks entity value increase), deferred compensation, and other long-term incentive plans.

> ### PRACTICAL TIP
>
> *The absence of stock makes incentive compensation for management a little more complicated. Executive management often requests bonus compensation based on profitability. This works in the short term, but does not give incentives for longer-term strategy implementation or growth. Typically, the goals for the executive team are the same as the strategic goals of the cooperative. Cooperatives are encouraged to consult with executive compensation counsel to design incentive plans that will attract needed talent, and ensure their interest are aligned with those of the cooperative.*

Section 8.4   Special Role Between Board and Staff

Cooperatives are, by definition, organizations in which the primary customers are also the entity's owners. Board members often have a complicated relationship with the cooperative's paid staff, because they are the supervisor, customer, and often friend of the staff members. For most other types of companies, board members supervise and provide feedback to only one individual: the Chief Executive Officer. Cooperative boards, too, should act only through the CEO. This is often difficult in practical terms, since the board has regular contact with staff in their customer role.

In addition, board members have fiduciary duties to the general membership, as described above. This includes a duty to avoid conflicts of interest and not to usurp corporate opportunities. Board members should be careful to ensure they do not receive special financial arrangements from the staff due to their position on the board.

APPENDIX A

COOPERATIVES STATUTES
ACROSS THE UNITED STATES

State	Statute
Alabama	AL ST § 2-10-1, *et seq.*
	AL ST § 10A-11-1.0, *et seq.*
	AL ST § 5-17-1, *et seq.*
	AL ST § 37-6-1, *et seq.*
	AL ST § 27-27-1, *et seq.*
Alaska	AK ST § 10.15.005, *et seq.*
	AK ST § 06.45.020, *et seq.*
	AK ST § 10.25.010, *et seq.*
	AK ST § 10.30.010, *et seq.*
Arizona	AZ ST § 10-2001, *et seq.*
	AZ ST § 6-501, *et seq.*
	AZ ST § 10-2051, *et seq.*
	AZ ST § 10-2121, *et seq.*
	AZ ST § 20-701, *et seq.*
Arkansas	AR ST § 2-2-101, *et seq.*
	AR ST § 4-30-101, *et seq.*
	AR ST § 23-17-201, *et seq.*
	AR ST § 23-4-901, *et seq.*
	AR ST § 23-18-301, *et seq.*
	AR ST § 23-35-101, *et seq.*
	AR ST § 20-77-1501, *et seq.*
	AR ST § 23-69-101, *et seq.*
	AR ST § 6-13-1001, *et seq.*
	AR ST § 4-30-201, *et seq.*
California	CA CORP § 12201, *et seq.*
	CA FOOD & AG §54036, § 54061,
	§ 54081, § 54082, § 54401, *et seq.*
	CA NONPROFIT COOP § 54001, *et*
	seq.

State	Statute
	CA WORKERS COOP § 12200, *et seq.*
	CA CREDIT UNION § 14000, *et seq.*
	CA ELECTRICAL COOP § 2776, *et seq*, § 3001, *et seq.*
	CA MUTUAL INSURANCE § 4010, *et seq.*
	CA COOP AND HOUSING § 817, *et seq.*
	CA FISH MARKETING § 13200, *et seq.*
Colorado	CO ST § 7-55-101, *et seq.*
	CO ST § 7-56-209, *et seq.*
	CO ST § 7-58-101, *et seq.*
	CO ST § 40-9.5-101, *et seq.*
	CO ST § 11-30-101, *et seq.*
	CO ST § 10-12-101, *et seq.*
	CO ST § 10-16-1004, *et seq.*
	CO ST § 38-33.5-101, *et seq.*
	CO ST § 7-56-210
Connecticut	CT ST § 33-183, *et seq.*
Delaware	DE ST TI 3 § 8501, *et seq.*
	DE ST TI 6 § 1401, *et seq.*
District of Columbia	DC CODE § 29-901, *et seq.*
Florida	FL ST § 618.01 , *et seq.*
Georgia	GA ST § 2-10-80, *et seq.*
Hawaii	HI ST § 421-1, *et seq.*
	HI ST § 421C-1, *et seq.*
Idaho	ID ST § 22-2601, *et seq.*
Illinois	IL ST CH 805 § 310/1, *et seq.*
Indiana	IN ST 15-12-1-1, *et seq.*
Iowa	IA ST § 497.1, *et seq.*
	IA ST § 501A.101, *et seq.*

State	Statute
Kansas	KS ST 17-1501, *et seq.*
Kentucky	KY ST § 272.010, *et seq.*
Louisiana	LA R.S. 3:71, *et seq.*
Maine	ME ST T. 13 § 1501, *et seq.*
Maryland	MD CORP & ASSNS § 5-501, *et seq.*
Massachusetts	MA ST 157 § 1, *et seq.*
Michigan	MI ST 450.98, *et seq.*
Minnesota	MN ST § 308A.001, *et seq.*
Mississippi	MS ST § 79-19-1, *et seq.*
Missouri	MO ST 274.010, *et seq.*
	MO ST 351.1000, *et seq.*
	MO ST 357.010, *et seq.*
Montana	MT ST 35-15-101, *et seq.*
Nebraska	NE ST § 21-1301, *et seq.*
Nevada	NV ST 81.010, *et seq.*
New Hampshire	NH ST § 301-A:1, *et seq.*
New Jersey	NJ ST 4:13-1, *et seq.*
	NJ ST 34:17-1, *et seq.*
New Mexico	NM ST § 53-4-1, *et seq.*
	NM ST § 76-12-1, *et seq.*
New York	NY COOP CORP § 1, *et seq.*
North Carolina	NC ST § 54-111, *et seq.*
North Dakota	ND ST 10-15-01, *et seq.*
Ohio	OH ST § 1729.01, *et seq.*
Oklahoma	OK ST T. 2 § 17-1, *et seq.*
	OK ST T. 18 § 421, *et seq.*
Oregon	OR ST § 62.015, *et seq.*
	OR ST § 646.030
Pennsylvania	15 Pa.C.S.A. § 7101, *et seq.*
	15 Pa.C.S.A. § 7501, *et seq.*
	31 PA ST § 700j-809
Rhode Island	RI ST § 7-7-1, *et seq.*
South Carolina	SC ST § 33-45-10, *et seq.*

State	Statute
South Dakota	SD ST § 47-15-1, *et seq.*
Tennessee	TN ST § 43-16-101, *et seq.*
	TN ST § 43-38-103, *et seq.*
	TN ST § 44-14-103
Texas	TX AGRIC § 52.001, *et seq.*
	TX BUS ORG § 2.011, § 2.110, § 2.111
	TX BUS ORG § 251.001, *et seq.*
Utah	UT ST § 3-1-1, *et seq.*
	UT ST § 16-6a-207
Vermont	VT ST T. 11 § 981, *et seq.*
Virginia	VA ST § 13.1-301, *et seq.*
Washington	RCW 23.78.010, *et seq.*
	RCW 23.86.007, *et seq.*
	RCW 24.06, *et seq.*
West Virginia	WV ST § 19-4-1, *et seq.*
Wisconsin	WI ST 185.01, *et seq.*
Wyoming	WY ST § 17-10-101, *et seq.*
Guam	18 G.C.A. § 13101, *et seq.*
Puerto Rico	5 L.P.R.A. § 4381, *et seq.*
Virgin Islands	13 V.I.C. § 551, *et seq.*

APPENDIX B

UNIFORM LIMITED COOPERATIVE ASSOCIATION ACT (2007)

Jurisdictions Wherein Act Has Been Adopted

Jurisdiction	Statutory Citation
Colorado	West's C.R.S.A. §§ 7-58-101 to 7-58-1704.
District of Columbia	DC Code §§ 29-1001.01 to 29-1015.08.
Kentucky	KRS §§ 272A.1-010 to 272A.17-040.
Nebraska	R.R.S. 1943, §§ 21-2901 to 21-29,134.
Oklahoma	18 Okl.St.Ann. §§ 441-101 to 441-1704.
Utah	U.C.A.1953, 16-16-101 to 16-16-1703.
Vermont	11C V.S.A. §§ 101 to 1703.
Washington	RCW 23.100.1302 to 1314.

APPENDIX C

EXAMPLE POSITION DESCRIPTION
BOARD OF DIRECTORS[287]

Title: Member, Board of Directors

Supervisor's Title: Members

JOB SUMMARY

A director has no authority to supervise as an individual director or to act independently on matters that should be acted upon by the board. Directors maintain working relationships with each other, the secretary, and CEO. The responsibilities and authority of the board of directors is executed within the limits established in the Articles, the Bylaws, federal and state statutes, and the objectives and policies established or authorized by the board of directors.

RESPONSIBILITIES AND DUTIES

A. Duties

- Be familiar with the Articles of Incorporation and Bylaws of the cooperative and conduct business in accordance with their provisions.

- Become familiar with federal/state laws under which the cooperative was incorporated.

- Understand the general legal responsibility of serving on the board of directors.

- Serve on committees and any special study groups as appointed by the chair of the board.[288]

- Attend outside and other special meetings as authorized by the board chairman.

- Maintain regular contact with members. Ensure that member complaints and/or suggestions are sympathetically considered; that members are kept adequately informed of

---

[287] This sample is provided courtesy of Harvey A. Meier, Harvey A. Meier, Ph.D., CMC, President, Harvey A. Meier Co. www.harveymeier.com.

[288] *See, e.g.,* CAL. CORP. CODE § 12352.

the affairs of the cooperative; and that sound relationships, understanding, and communication are maintained among the board, management and members.

- Advise the board chair/president or board of significant information or issues that could affect the cooperative.

- Be responsive to ideas and proposals that are m the interest of the cooperative and member needs.

- Review and evaluate all data, reports, etc. provided to them relevant to board matters.

- Stay abreast of industry information and trends.

- Participate in director training programs.

- Attend member meetings and annual meetings and participate when required.

- Supervise the CEO.

B. Responsibilities

- Select CEO; determine salary, duties and authority and review performance at least annually.

- Adopt board policies relating to governance of the cooperative and for guidance of management.

- Develop (with the CEO) and adopt long-range business strategies and plans.

- Facilitate board elections and the election of board officers.

- Fill board vacancies.

- Approve annual operating plans and other significant commitments that affect the cooperative's financial results.

- Require and review monthly financial and operating reports. Exercise control over the cooperative's activities through the review of these reports, analyses, and statistics submitted by the CEO and effect remedial action through the CEO whenever the need is indicated.

- Annually require legal counsel to review minutes of board meetings, contracts, and other corporate documents to confirm consistency of board decisions with Articles of Incorporation and Bylaws. Provide legal counsel with a copy of the monthly board meeting agenda and minutes.

- Retain auditor to prepare actual financial statements, issue an opinion thereon. report these in person to the board, and to issue a management letter to the board. Provide the auditor with access to a copy of the monthly board meeting minutes.

- Determine patronage dividend disbursements and all other matters related to member equity issues in collaboration with management.

- Understand terms of all significant contracts requiring board approval (leases, loan agreements, other, etc.) into which the cooperative has entered.

- Hold regular monthly/quarterly board meetings.

- Abide by and support all decisions reached by a majority of the board as if they were unanimous.

- Avoid contacting individual employees about matters pertaining to the operations of the company. These should be discussed with the CEO only.

- Board executive session business should not be discussed with non-board members.

- Direct the CEO to provide for adequate insurance coverage of company assets including commercial, health and medical, fidelity bonding, director and officer liability coverage, etc.

LIMITATIONS AND COLLABORATION

The board does not engage in the operation or day-to-day management of the company. By delegating and approving management programs and actions, the board plans and controls the overall course and performance of the company. The board can replace the CEO if it believes performance is unsatisfactory: however, the board must not supplant management by trying to do management's job itself. Decisions can be made solely by the board, made by management, or shared by both. Despite efforts to designate distinct areas, in many respects, decisions require a team effort – a collaborative effort so to speak – between the board and the CEO. Examples of decisions to be made solely by the board, and those made solely by the CEO, or shared by both panics are as follows:

Board Decisions Solely

- Defining corporate objectives, policies, and goals (however, with management participation and recommendations).

- Electing board and corporate officers including the chair, vice chair, secretary, and treasurer.

- Long-term financial commitments including sources and types of financing with management input.

- Selection of CEO and setting her/his salary. Defining duties of the CEO.

- Employing an independent auditing firm. Retaining board legal counsel.

- Filling board position vacancies.

- Make basic changes in financial structure with management input.

- Approval of major plans and commitments. Matters where member decisions are required.

- Approval of the employee retirement and banality program(s).

Management Decisions Primarily

- Basic relationships with the suppliers/vendors/ customers.

- Defining operating or management level objectives, goals and policies. Short-term commitment of resources.

- Preparation of budgets, acquisition/disposition plans, board.

- Manufacturing/production plans, asset and marketing plans for approval by the board.

- Defining duties of division managers/department heads.

- Administration of the employee-benefits program, salary/wage, and employee performance evaluation programs consistent with salary scales approved by the board.

- Selection and/or disciplining of employees. Resolution of employee grievances. Measurements of employee performance. Selection of legal counsel to management.

- Employee working conditions.

Shared Decision Areas

- Determination and selection of bank, insurance, and benefit needs, plans and programs.

- Relations with government, industry and general public.

- Amounts and sources of working capital.

- Engaging selected professional services (*e.g.*, legal counsel, consultant) for matters pertaining to joint decision making areas.

- Selection of bank depositories.

- Appraisal of the cooperative's performance. Distribution of earnings.

- Employee bonding.

- Issuing capital instruments.

- Changes in basic organizational structure. Authorizing facility construction, expansion, etc.

- Capital expenditures exceeding pre-defined CEO authority limits authorized for facility construction, expansion/replacements.

APPENDIX D

[COMPANY]
CODE OF BUSINESS CONDUCT AND ETHICS

[Company] ("[Company Initials]") is committed to the highest standards of legal and ethical business conduct. This Code of Business Conduct and Ethics summarizes the legal, ethical and regulatory standards that [Company] must follow and is a reminder to our directors, officers and employees, of the seriousness of that commitment. Compliance with this Code and high standards of business conduct is mandatory for every [Company] employee.

INTRODUCTION

Our business is becoming increasingly complex, both in terms of the geographies in which we function and the laws with which we must comply. To help our directors, officers and employees understand what is expected of them and to carry out their responsibilities, we have created this Code of Business Conduct and Ethics. It is the responsibility of [Company]'s President and Chief Executive Officer ("CEO") to oversee adherence to the Code.

This Code is not intended to be a comprehensive guide to all of our policies or to all your responsibilities under law or regulation. It provides general parameters to help you resolve the ethical and legal issues you encounter in conducting our business. Think of this Code as a guideline, or a minimum requirement, that must always be followed. If you have any questions about anything in the Code or appropriate actions in light of the Code, you may contact the CEO or the Chairman of the Board of Directors.

We expect each of our directors, officers and employees to read and become familiar with the ethical standards described in this Code and to affirm your agreement to adhere to these standards by signing the Compliance Certificate that appears at the end of this Code. Violations of the law, our corporate policies, or this Code may lead to disciplinary action, including dismissal.

I. We Insist on Honest and Ethical Conduct By All of Our Directors, Officers, Employees and Other Representatives

- We have built our business based on excellence in products and services: but quality employees and representatives who adhere to the very highest standards of honesty, ethics and fairness in our dealings with all of our business contacts. We place the highest value on the integrity of our directors, our officers and our employees and demand this level of integrity in all our dealings. We insist on not only ethical dealings with others, but on the ethical handling of actual or apparent conflicts of interest between personal and professional relationships.

Fair Dealing

Directors, officers and employees are required to deal honestly and fairly with our customers, suppliers, competitors and other third parties.

Sales are the lifeblood of any organization. We market our products and services fairly and vigorously based on our honesty, creativity and ingenuity and the proven quality of the products. Serving our customers effectively is our most important goal-in the eyes of the customer you are [Company]. In our dealings with customers and suppliers, we:

- prohibit bribes, kickbacks or any other form of improper payment, direct or indirect, to any representative of government, labor union, customer or supplier in order to obtain a contract, some other commercial benefit or government action;

- prohibit our directors, officers and employees from accepting any bribe, kickback or improper payment from anyone;

- prohibit gifts or favors of more than nominal value to or from our customers or suppliers;

- limit marketing and client entertainment expenditures to those that are necessary, prudent, job-related and consistent with our policies;

- require clear and precise communication in our contracts, our advertising, our literature, and our other public statements and seek to eliminate misstatement of fact or misleading impressions;

- reflect accurately on all invoices to customers the sale price and terms of sales for products sold or services rendered;

- protect all proprietary data our customers or suppliers provide to us as reflected in our agreements with them;

- prohibit our representatives from otherwise taking unfair advantage of our customers or suppliers, or other third parties, through manipulation, concealment, abuse of privileged information or any other unfair-dealing practice.

Conflicts of Interest; Corporate Opportunities

Our directors, officers and employees should not be involved in any activity that creates or gives the appearance of a conflict of interest between their personal interests and the interests of [Company]. In particular, without the specific permission of our CEO, no director, officer or employee shall:

- be a consultant to, or a director, officer or employee of, or otherwise operate an outside business that:

  o markets products or services in competition with our current or potential products and services;

  o supplies products or services to [Company] (other than directors whose furs are marketed through [Company] on the same terms and conditions as any other producer);

  o purchases products or services from [Company] (other than directors whose furs are marketed through [Company] on the same terms and conditions as any other producer); or

  o have any financial interest, including significant stock ownership, in any entity with which we do business that might create or give the appearance of a conflict of interest;

- seek or accept any personal loan or services from any entity with which we do business, except from financial institutions or service providers offering similar loans or services to third parties under similar terms in the ordinary course of their respective businesses;

- be a consultant to, or a director, officer or employee of, or otherwise operate an outside business if the demands of the outside business would interfere with the director's, officer's or employee's responsibilities to us, (if in doubt, consult your supervisor or the CEO or the Chairman);

- accept any personal loan or guarantee of obligations from [Company], (other than pelt advances or loans made through [Company]'s relationships with financial institutions in which the decision to lend is made by the financial institution with no influence by [Company]), or conduct business on behalf of [Company] with immediate family members, which include spouses, children, parents, siblings and persons sharing the same home whether or not legal relatives.

Directors, officers, and employees must notify the CEO or Chairman of the Board of the existence of any actual or potential conflict of interest.

Confidentiality and Corporate Assets

Our directors, officers and employees are entrusted with our confidential information and with the confidential information of our suppliers, customers or other business partners. This information may include (1) technical or scientific information about current and future products, services or research, (2) business or marketing plans or projections, (3) earnings and other internal financial data, (4) personnel information, (5) supply and customer lists and (6) other non-public information that, if disclosed, might be of use to our competitors, or harmful to our suppliers, customers or other business partners. This information is [Company]'s property or the property of [Company]'s suppliers, customers or business partners and in many cases was developed at great expense. Our directors, officers and employees shall:

- Not discuss confidential information with or in the presence of any unauthorized persons, including family members and friends;

- Use confidential information only for our legitimate business purposes and not for personal gain;

- Not disclose confidential information to third parties.

- Not use [Company] property or resources for any personal benefit or the personal benefit of anyone else. [Company] property includes the [Company] internet, email, and voicemail services, which should be used only for business related activities, and which may be monitored by [Company] at any time without notice.

II. We Provide Full, Fair, Accurate, Timely and Understandable Disclosure

We are committed to providing our shareholders and bankers with full, fair, accurate, timely and understandable disclosure in the reports that provide to them. To this end, our directors, officers and employees shall:

- not make false or misleading entries in our books and records for any reason;

- not condone any undisclosed or unrecorded bank accounts or assets established for any purpose;

- comply with generally accepted accounting principles at all times;

- notify our Chief Financial Officer if there is an unreported transaction;

- maintain a system of internal accounting controls that will provide reasonable assurances to management that all transactions are properly recorded;

- maintain books and records that accurately and fairly reflect our transactions;

- prohibit the establishment of any undisclosed or unrecorded funds or assets;

- maintain a system of internal controls that will provide reasonable assurances to our management that material information about [Company] is made known to management, particularly during the periods in which our periodic reports are being prepared;

- present information in a clear and orderly manner and avoid the use of unnecessary legal and financial language in our periodic reports; and

- not communicate to the public any non-public information except through our Chief Financial Officer or CEO.

III. We Comply With all Laws, Rules and Regulations

We will comply with all laws and governmental regulations that are applicable to our activities, and expect all our directors, officers and employees to obey the law. Specifically, we are committed to:

- maintaining a safe and healthy work environment;

- promoting a workplace that is free from discrimination or harassment based on race, color, religion, sex, age, national origin, disability or other factors that are unrelated to the [Company]'s business interests;

- supporting fair competition and laws prohibiting restraints of trade and other unfair trade practices;

- conducting our activities in full compliance with all applicable environmental laws;

- keeping the political activities of our directors, officers and employees separate from our business;

- prohibiting any illegal payments, gifts, or gratuities to any government officials or political party;

- prohibiting the unauthorized use, reproduction, or distribution of any third party's trade secrets, copyrighted information or confidential information, and

- complying with all applicable state and federal securities laws.

REPORTING AND EFFECT OF VIOLATIONS

Compliance with this code of conduct is, first and foremost, the individual responsibility of every director, officer and employee. We attempt to foster a work environment in which ethical issues and concerns may be raised and discussed with supervisors or with others without the fear of retribution. It is our responsibility to provide a system of reporting and access when you wish to report a suspected violation, or to seek counseling, and the normal chain of command cannot, for whatever reason, be used.

Administration

Our Board of Directors has established the standards of business conduct contained in this Code and oversees compliance with this Code. Training on this code will be included in the orientation of new employees and provided to existing directors, officers, and employees on an on-going basis. To ensure familiarity with the Code, directors, officers, and employees will be asked to read the Code and sign a Compliance Certificate annually.

Reporting Violations and Questions

Directors, officers, and employees must report, in person or in writing, any known or suspected violations of laws, governmental regulations or this Code to the CEO or the Chairman of the Board of Directors. Additionally, directors, officers, and employees may contact them with a question or concern about this Code or a business practice. Any questions or violation reports will be addressed immediately and seriously, and can be made anonymously. If you feel uncomfortable reporting suspected violations to these individuals, you may report matters to [Corporate Counsel], our outside counsel. The address and telephone number of these individuals are listed in the attachment to this Code.

[Company] will not allow any retaliation against a director, officer or employee who acts in good faith in reporting any violation.

Our outside counsel will investigate any reported violations and will determine an appropriate response, including corrective action and preventative measures, involving the Chairman of the Board of Directors or the CEO when required. All reports will be treated confidentially to every extent possible.

Consequences of a Violation

Directors, officers and employees that violate any laws, governmental regulations or this Code will face appropriate, case specific disciplinary action, which may include demotion or immediate discharge.

Names and Addresses (as of [include date of information])

Reporting Contacts:

[Ethics Officer]:

Name:_____

The Chair of our Audit Committee:

Name:_____

Address:_____   Address:_____

_____   _____

_____   _____

Phone:_____   Phone:_____
E-mail:_____   E-mail:_____

Reporting Contacts:

Name, address, phone, and e-   Name, address, phone and e-
mail   mail

Additional Reporting Contact:

       Our Outside Counsel:

       _____, Esq.

       Dorsey & Whitney LLP

       [address, phone and e-mail address]

COMPLIANCE CERTIFICATE

I have read and understand the [Company] Code of Business Conduct and Ethics (the "**Code**"). I will adhere in all respects to the ethical standards described in the Code. I further confirm my understanding that any violation of the Code will subject me to appropriate disciplinary action, which may include demotion or discharge.

I certify to [Company] that I am not in violation of the Code, unless I have noted such violation in a signed Statement of Exceptions attached to this Compliance Certificate.

Date:_____   _____

Name:_____
Title Position:_____

Check one of the following:

☐ A Statement of Exceptions is attached.

☐ No Statement of Exceptions is attached.

APPENDIX E

RESTRICTIONS ON USE OF "COOPERATIVE" IN ENTITY NAME

State	Statute
Alabama	ALA CODE § 2-10-1 (2020) regulates the use of the word "cooperative" for cooperative associations marketing agricultural products.
	ALA CODE § 37-6-43 (2020) regulates the use of the word "cooperative" for electric cooperatives.
Alaska	ALASKA STAT. § 10.15.575 (2020).
Arizona	ARIZ. REV. STAT. § 10-2054 (2020) regulates the use of the word "cooperative" for electric cooperative nonprofit membership corporations.
	ARIZ. REV. STAT. § 10-2124 (2020) for nonprofit electric generation and transmission cooperative corporations.
Arkansas	Cooperatives are regulated in ARK. CODE §§ 4-30-101 − 4-30-207 (2020).
California	CAL CORP. CODE § 12311(b).
Colorado	COLO. CODE REGS. § 7-55-111 (repealed 2004).
Connecticut	Cooperatives are regulated in CONN. GEN STAT. §§ 33-183 − 33-217 (2020).
Delaware	DEL. CODE ANN. tit. 3, §§ 8501 − 8562 (2020) regulate cooperative agricultural associations.
	DEL. CODE ANN. tit. 6, §§ 1401 − 1414 (2020) regulate workers cooperatives.
District of Columbia	Cooperatives are regulated in D.C. CODE §§ 29-901 − 29-1015 (2020).
Florida	FLA. STAT. § 425.05 (2020) regulates the use of the term for rural electric cooperatives.

State	Statute
	FLA. STAT. § 618.27(1) (2020) regulates the use of the term for agricultural cooperative marketing associations.
Georgia	GA. CODE ANN. § 2-10-111 (2020) regulates Cooperative Marketing Associations. GA. CODE ANN. (2020) does not regulate any other type of cooperative association.
Hawaii	HAW. REV. STAT. § 421C-34 (2020).
Idaho	IDAHO CODE ANN. §§ 22-2601 - 22-2627 (2020) regulates cooperative marketing associations. IDAHO CODE ANN. (2020) does not regulate any other type of cooperative association.
Illinois	805 ILL. COMP. STAT 310 / 22 (2020).
Indiana	IND. CODE § 15-12-1-40 (2020) regulates the use of the term "cooperative" for agricultural cooperatives.
Iowa	IOWA CODE § 497.30 (2020).
Kansas	KANSAS STAT. ANN. § 17-1515 (2020) regulates the name of the term "cooperative" for cooperative societies. KANSAS STAT. ANN. § 17-1627 (2020) regulates the name of the term "cooperative" for cooperative marketing corporations. KANSAS STAT. ANN. § 17-4655 (2020) regulates the name of the term "cooperative" for electric cooperatives.
Kentucky	KY. REV. STAT. ANN. §§ 272.990, 272.044 (2020).
Louisiana	LA. REV. STAT. ANN. § 17:2805 § 3:140 (2020).
Maine	ME. REV. STAT. tit. 13, § 1744 (2020) regulates Cooperative Affordable Housing Ownership.

State	Statute
	ME. REV. STAT. tit. 13, § 1976 (2020) regulates Employee Cooperative Corporations.
Maryland	MD. CODE. ANN. CORPORATIONS AND ASSOCIATIONS § 5-510 (2020).
Massachusetts	MASS. GEN. LAWS ANN. ch. 157, § 3, § 8 (2020).
Michigan	MICH. COMP. LAWS § 450.3123 (2020).
Minnesota	MINN. STAT. § 308A.011 subdiv. 1 (2020).
Mississippi	MISS. CODE ANN. § 79-19-39 (2020).
Missouri	MO. REV. STAT. § 357.190.1 (2020).
Montana	MONT. CODE ANN. §69-8-311 (2020) regulate cooperative utilities. They are the only kind of cooperatives regulated in MON. CODE. ANN (2020).
Nebraska	NEB. REV. STAT. § 21-1306 (2020).
Nevada	NEV. REV. STAT. § 81.170 – 81.270 (2020) regulate cooperative associations.
New Hampshire	N.H. REV. STAT. ANN. § 301-43-A (2020).
New Jersey	Corporations are regulated in N.J. REV. STAT. §§ 14A:1-1 – 15A:16-2 (2020). Cooperative agricultural associations are regulated in § 4:11-17.
New Mexico	N.M STAT. ANN. 53-4-37(A) (2020).
New York	N.Y. COOPERATIVE CORPORATIONS LAW § 3(j) (2020).
North Carolina	N.C. GEN. STAT. § 54-139 (2020).
North Dakota	N.D. CENT CODE § 10-15-58 (2020).
Ohio	OHIO REV. CODE ANN. § 1729.04(B) (2020).
Oklahoma	OKLA. STAT. tit. 18, § 435 (20120).
Oregon	OR. REV. STAT. § 62.850(1) (2020).
Pennsylvania	15 PA. CONS. STAT. § 7103 (2020).
Rhode Island	R.I. GEN. LAWS ANN. § 7-8-33 (West 2020).
South Carolina	S.C. CODE ANN. § 33-45-20 (2020).
South Dakota	S.D. CODE ANN. § 47-15-42 (2020).
Tennessee	TENN. CODE ANN. § 43-38-105 (2020).

State	Statute
Texas	TEX. BUSINESS ORGANIZATIONS CODE ANN. § 251.452(a) (2020).
Utah	UTAH CODE ANN. § 3-1-23 (2020).
Vermont	VT. STAT. ANN. tit 11, § 992 (2020).
Virginia	VA. CODE ANN. § 13.1-308(A) (2020).
Washington	Wash. Rev. Code § 23.86.030(2) (2020).
West Virginia	W. VA. CODE §19-4-21 (2020).
Wisconsin	WIS. STAT. §§ 185.94, 193.105 (2020).
Wyoming	WYO. STAT. ANN. §17-10-207 (2020) regulates the name of cooperative marketing associations, which are the only cooperative corporations regulated.

TABLE OF AUTHORITIES

STATUTES

OTHER AUTHORITIES

INDEX

About the Author

Michael W. Droke, a partner in the Seattle office of the law firm of Dorsey & Whitney LLP, has represented agricultural and other cooperatives for almost 30 years. He is an active member of Dorsey's national Food, Beverages, and Agribusiness industry group and the Cooperative Law practice group. Mike currently serves as the outside general counsel to a national consumer cooperative and, additionally, one of the largest agricultural cooperatives in Washington State. He assists cooperatives in a wide array of legal issues, from business law, employment matters, and executive compensation to trademarks and dispute resolution. He is licensed in California and Washington, and is the primary author and editor of this guide.

Contributing Editors

David P. Swanson, a partner in Dorsey's Minneapolis office, currently serves as Co-Chair of the Cooperative Law practice group. For more than 30 years, his practice has focused primarily on organizations structured as cooperatives, assisting with legal issues unique to cooperatives, including tax and securities matters. Dave also assists clients with organizational issues, project development, financing and transactions. His client base spans numerous cooperative sectors, including food and agricultural, rural electric cooperatives, consumer cooperatives and purchasing cooperatives, as well as cooperative financial institutions. Dave serves on the boards of several cooperatives and cooperative-oriented nonprofits.

Michael A. Lindsay is a partner in the Minneapolis office of Dorsey & Whitney. He currently serves as Co-

Chair of the firm-wide Commercial Litigation practice, Co-Chair of the Antitrust practice and as an active member of the Cooperatives practice group. Michael practices in the area of general civil litigation, with a strong emphasis on antitrust (litigation and counseling) and other commercial litigation.

Christopher R. Duggan is a senior tax attorney in Dorsey's Minneapolis office and serves as a member of the firm's Cooperatives practice group. Chris advises clients on minimizing state and local income, sales and use, excise, and business and occupation tax exposure. Chris also assists clients with federal tax issues, audits and appeals, and has special expertise in Section 1031 exchanges, federal excise taxes, and federal tax credits, such as the New Markets Tax Credit. For over 15 years, Chris has advised and assisted cooperative associations with tax issues relating to cooperative operation and distributions, restructurings, recapitalizations, mergers and joint ventures. Chris has also assisted clients in converting to and from cooperative status.

Rachel Benedict is a corporate associate in Dorsey's Minneapolis office. She represents both buyers and sellers in a variety of transactions, including divestitures, asset purchases, stock purchases and mergers. Rachel also advises clients on a range of corporate governance, equity incentive compensation, commercial contracting and general corporate matters. She has worked on complex transactions in various industries, including agriculture, energy, health and technology.

Kendall Fisher is an associate in Dorsey's Seattle office and member of both the Tax and Cooperatives practice groups. His practice focuses on U.S. federal tax issues related to domestic and cross-border mergers, acquisitions and debt and equity financings, as well as inbound and outbound tax planning related to multinational structures, tax treaties, controlled foreign corporation issues, passive foreign investment company issues, the Foreign Account Tax Compliance Act (FATCA), and the Foreign Investment in Real Property Tax Act (FIRPTA). His practice also includes domestic business formations, joint ventures, acquisitions, combinations, sales, and general tax planning. Kendall also regularly advises on tax issues related to cooperative formations and restructurings.

For questions or to provide feedback about this book, please contact Mike Droke at:

Droke.Michael@dorsey.com or (206) 903-8709.

About Dorsey & Whitney LLP

For over 100 years, Dorsey & Whitney has provided practical advice and legal defense to premier companies. With over 550 lawyers in 19 offices across three continents, Dorsey offers full-service legal expertise to clients across dozens of industries, in every stage of development, virtually anywhere in the world.

Dorsey & Whitney's Cooperatives practice group is a recognized national leader in the field of cooperative law. The team has more than 25 professionals representing cooperative organizations across the nation from a wide variety of co-op sectors, including agriculture, energy and utilities, purchasing, housing, professional services, and healthcare, among others. Dorsey also represents other agriculture-related organizations, such as commodity promotion groups, cooperative banks, and cooperative trade associations. Dorsey's Co-op team has also organized or advised many purchasing or shared services cooperatives and has frequently helped companies considering joining a cooperative. The team has worked with cooperatives that provide all kinds of goods or services, from mushrooms, bicycles, or computer software to agricultural laborers or funeral homes.

Dorsey's Co-op practice group comprises a full-service team of lawyers with a wide range of practice area expertise, including project development and finance, mergers and acquisitions, real estate, labor, employment and employee benefits, environmental, land use and permits, securities, international and trade regulations, construction contracts, trademark and branding, intellectual property and licensing, FERC and other regulatory matters, plus many areas unique to cooperatives, including formation and organization, voting rights and governance issues, antitrust/Capper-Volstead Act, and tax is-sues.

While the firm is truly global in location and size, many of Dorsey's Co-op attorneys hail from the country's rural heartland, offering the team a true understanding of the needs of rural America. Clients benefit from Dorsey's combination of hands-on, local support plus the "big city" experience and sophisticated resources required to assist with the complex legal and business issues that often arise as cooperative organizations grow. The team has seen first-hand the economic benefits enjoyed by the cooperatives they have organized, as well as the unique legal challenges their co-op clients sometimes face, and they know what needs to be done in order for the cooperative and its members to be successful.

Dorsey & Whitney LLP
www.dorsey.com

USA

Anchorage
1031 W. 4th Ave, Ste 600
Anchorage, AK 99501
(907) 276-4557
Anchorage@Dorsey.com

Dallas
300 Crescent Court, Ste 400
Dallas, TX 75201
(214) 981-9900
Dallas@Dorsey.com

Denver
1400 Wewatta St, Ste 400
Denver, CO 80202
(303) 629-3400
Denver@Dorsey.com

Des Moines
801 Grand, Ste 4100
Des Moines, IA 50309
(515) 283-1000
DesMoines@Dorsey.com

Minneapolis
50 S. Sixth St., Ste 1500
Minneapolis, MN 55402
(612)340-2600
Minneapolis@Dorsey.com

Missoula
125 Bank St, Ste 600
Missoula, MT 59802
(406) 721-6025
Missoula@Dorsey.com

New York
51 West 52nd Street
New York, NY 10019
(212) 415-9200
NewYork@Dorsey.com

Palo Alto
305 Lytton Avenue
Palo Alto, CA 94301
(650) 857-1717
PaloAlto@Dorsey.com

Salt Lake City
111 South Main St., Ste 2100
Salt Lake City, UT 84111
(801) 933-7360
SaltLakeCity@Dorsey.com

Seattle
701 Fifth Avenue, Ste 6100
Seattle, WA 98104
(206) 903-8800
Seattle@Dorsey.com

Southern California
600 Anton Blvd, Ste 2000
Costa Mesa, CA 92626
(714) 800-1400
SoCal@Dorsey.com

Washington, DC
1401 New York Ave NW, Ste 900
Washington, DC 20006
(202) 442-3000
WashingtonDC@Dorsey.com

Wilmington
300 Delaware Ave, Ste 1010
Wilmington, DE 19801
(302) 425-7171
Delaware@Dorsey.com

CANADA

Toronto
Brookfield Place
161 Bay Street, Ste 4310
Toronto, ON M5J 2S1
(416) 367-7370
Toronto@Dorsey.com

Vancouver
1095 West Pender St, Ste 1070
Vancouver, BC V6E 2M6
(604) 687-5151
Vancouver@dorsey.com

EUROPE

London
199 Bishopsgate
London EC2M 3UT
England
44 (0)20 7031 3700
London@Dorsey.com

ASIA-PACIFIC

Beijing
Twin Towers (West), Suite 1101A
B12 Jianguomenwai Avenue
Chaoyang District, Beijing 100022
China
(86-10) 8513-5900
Beijing@Dorsey.com

Hong Kong
88 Queensway
Ste 3008, One Pacific Place
Hong Kong
China
(011-852) 2526-5000
HongKong@Dorsey.com

Shanghai
Ste 807- 808, Kerry Parkside
No. 1155 Fang Dian Road
Pudong, Shanghai 201204
China
(86-21) 6288-2323
Shanghai@Dorsey.com

Notes